Parks and Gardens of Avon

Parks and Gardens of Avon

Edited by
Stewart Harding and David Lambert

AVON GARDENS TRUST

First published in 1994 by
Avon Gardens Trust, 325 Fishponds Road, Bristol BS5 6QG

Text ©1994 Avon Gardens Trust

Illustrations ©1994 Owners listed on page vii

Designed, edited and produced for the Avon Gardens Trust by
Open Books Publishing Ltd, Beaumont House, Wells BA5 2LD,
Somerset

ISBN 0 7291 0230 0

Colour separation by Mandarin Offset Ltd, Hong Kong

Typesetting by PrePress Ltd

Printed in England by The Bath Press Ltd

Contents

Foreword

The text of this book is based on a first draft prepared by workers on the Avon Historic Gardens Survey in 1987–8, with sections written by Mike Dawson, Stewart Harding, Rob Iles, Steve Lanigan, Jane Root, Mary Stacey and Toby Thacker. In editing it, we have re-arranged the chapters into purely chronological divisions, and have updated them with new information. We are most grateful to the original authors for their agreement to this extensive revision of their text, and for their continuing advice and support. All errors are now our responsibility.

At Avon County Council, Mary Stacey spent a great deal of time editing the first version of the text, and has coordinated much of the work on this final version; we are grateful to her colleague Katie Porter for photographing a number of the illustrations; Jim Hill has redrawn several archaeological plans with great skill.

Patrick and Caroline Taylor of Open Books have brought the book into being. Their time in editing and designing it was freely given, and their patient expertise has been invaluable. Special thanks are owed to Dorothy Brown for her encouragement when the project looked fated never to succeed. We would also like to thank the following: Liz Bevan of Bath Reference Library, James Bond, Simon Bonvoisin of Nicholas Pearson Associates, Dominic Cole of Land Use Consultants, Hazel Conway, Jane Crawley, Lady Margaret Elton, David Eveleigh, Francis Greenacre and Karin Walton of Bristol City Museum, Deborah Jones and Wendy Pettigrew of the Countryside Commission, Nick Lee of Bristol University Library, David McLaughlin, Bill McNaught, Lorna McRobie, Tim Mowl, John Phibbs of Debois Landscape Survey Group, Margaret Richards the Badminton archivist, Susan Sloman of the Victoria Art Gallery in Bath, Peggy Stembridge, Nigel Temple, Christopher Woodward of the Buildings of Bath Museum. We are most grateful to Lindsay Smith of Avon County Planning Department who supported the work of the Avon Gardens Trust until his untimely death in February, 1994. We would also like to acknowledge all those who worked on the Avon Historic Gardens Survey between 1983 and 1988, and whose research forms the basis of the book.

The publication of this book has been made possible by generous grants from Avon County Council, the Ernest Cook Trust, the Stanley Smith Horticultural Trust, and Task Force Trees, a special unit of the Countryside Commission. We would like to express our appreciation of their support.

Stewart Harding and David Lambert

February 1994

Acknowledgements

The Avon Gardens Trust is extremely grateful to those listed below for much help in finding pictures and for permission to reproduce them. In a few cases we have been unable to trace copyright owners.

Avon County Council (Figs 1, 5, 9, 11, 12, 14,15, 16, 18, 19, 20; Plates 2, 13, 14, 17, 23, 25, 26, 30, 31, 33, 34, 38)
Bath Preservation Trust (Fig 36)
Bath Reference Library (Fig 59)
Her Grace the Duchess of Beaufort (Plate 7)
Bristol University Reference Library (Fig 39; Plates 20, 21, 22)
Dorothy Brown (Fig 10; Plate 5)
City of Bristol Museum and Art Gallery (Figs 27, 28, 32, 33, 34, 35, 37, 38, 48, 54, 57, 61; Plates 8, 11, 15, 19; Cover photograph)
Lady Elton (Figs 26, 49, 50)
Dr Stewart Harding (Figs 30, 41, 47, 53, 56, 58, 62; Plates 29, 39)
Rob Iles (Fig 3; Plate 1)
David Lambert (Figs 4, 6, 17, 31, 43, 44, 63; Plates 3, 4, 10, 12, 16, 18, 24, 27, 28, 32, 35, 36, 37, 40)
William McNaught (Fig 13)
Dr Tim Mowl (Plate 41)
Patrick Taylor (Plate 9)
Dr Karin Walton (Fig 22)

Chapter 1

Parks and Pleasances – Norman to Tudor

T HE HUNTING OF DEER and other game was a favourite pastime of
Anglo-Saxon kings, who hunted locally in the Mendips and probably in the
north of the county from their palace at Pucklechurch. But they simply hunted
wild deer across open countryside; the idea of royal forests and of enclosing deer
within parks was introduced by the Normans. Thirty-five parks are recorded in
the Domesday Book towards the end of the eleventh century, one of them at
Sodbury. Within a few years a royal park had been established at Alveston,
mentioned in 1130 when it was being enlarged. Other early parks are recorded at
Bath and Englishcombe, but the majority of the medieval parks in the county were
made in the thirteenth and fourteenth centuries.

Parks were a common feature of the medieval countryside of Avon (Fig. 1).
They were large enclosed areas of grassland and woodland, created for the keeping
of deer. Although significantly different both in terms of function and appearance
from later parks, they did, in one respect, serve a similar function to that of the
great landscape parks of more recent times: they were a very obvious and
ostentatious status symbol for the major landowners of their day.

It is often stated that Capability Brown and other landscape designers of the
eighteenth century 'swept away' earlier gardens and parks in England. However,
clean sweeps were not so easily achieved. Indeed, John Phibbs has argued that the
vestiges of earlier landscapes afforded an eighteenth-century park instant venera-
bility and pedigree, lumps and bumps in the ground along with ancient trees being
often deliberately retained. Thus many of the sites that were greatly altered in the
eighteenth century retain traces – sometimes dramatic – of their earlier layouts.

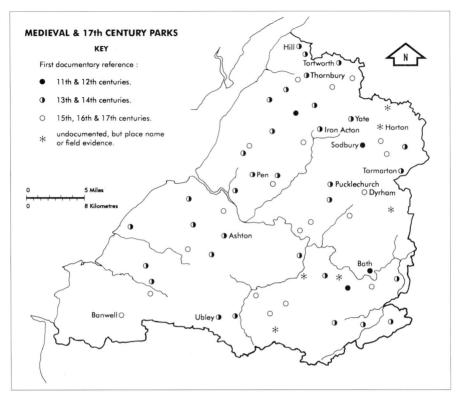

Fig. 1. Map of Avon showing the distribution of parks of various periods from the Middle Ages to the seventeenth century.

Royal forests and chases

The medieval park, enclosed with pales and a bank and ditch, complemented much larger open hunting grounds. The Normans had introduced the concept of Royal Forests, although these may have had their origins as Roman hunting grounds – a possibility given weight by the establishment of a medieval deer park around the Roman villa at Tockington. A royal forest involved not tree-planting but the imposition of ferocious controls (Forest Law) on the hunting of deer and other game over vast tracts of countryside, under which all rights over the deer and wild swine were reserved to the Crown. The areas concerned would include farmland, villages and farms, although the ownership of the land was not necessarily affected, and nor were the rights of common grazing. Associated with the royal forest were enclosures for deer, which is the origin of the name Dyrham, from the Saxon *deor-hamm*, probably one of the oldest deer parks in the country.

Given their size and number, the royal forests were only rarely hunted over by the monarch. More usually they were hunted by professionals, killing deer to royal order. There are records of royal orders of venison, requiring hundreds of deer from all over England. One, of July 1315, includes an order to the Constable of Bristol Castle to provide twelve bucks from Bristol (that is, Kingswood Chase) and sixteen bucks from Thornbury Park, then owned by the King.

Chases were slightly smaller areas over which similar controls were exercised by the King and by individual manorial lords. Being smaller, chases were more often hunted over for sport (Plate 1). Kingswood had been a royal forest covering some 200 square miles/518 square kilometres; in 1228 it was disafforested and a much smaller area, renamed Kingswood Chase, was kept by the king for hunting.

Deer

The deer in the thirty-five parks in Domesday would have been native red and roe deer, but parks proliferated after the introduction by the Normans of fallow deer, and this became by far the most common stock for parks (Plate 2). Records of sixteenth-century parks often mention small numbers of the native red deer. A survey of Eastwood Park at Thornbury records five hundred fallow and fifty red deer. The two types were sometimes physically separated within a park. Leland, writing in the 1540s, refers to two parks at Iron Acton, one for red deer and the other for fallow deer.

Fig. 2. A deer leap at Wolseley Park, Staffordshire, from a nineteenth-century engraving.

From the time of William I, all deer belonged to the Crown, but manorial lords frequently sought royal licence to hunt smaller game such as hares and rabbits. This was known as 'free warren', and there are numerous local examples. However, there are comparatively few recorded licences to enclose deer parks. Two notable new deer parks were those licensed at Siston (1252) and at Ashton (1392). New parks were often honoured with gifts of deer from the Crown. Many park pales had gaps, called deer leaps, which allowed wild deer to get in, but not then to

3

escape (Fig. 2). There were also specific formal arrangements. The licence for Siston allowed its owner, Robert Walerand, to keep any deer that entered from the nearby Kingswood Chase. In 1280 Richard de Aumari was allowed by the King to take five live bucks from Mendip Forest to replace five that had escaped from his park at Ubley.

Parks were not always hunting grounds. The average extent of ground was only about 250 acres/100 hectares, and parks were primarily larders with fresh meat kept in a convenient space that was small enough to make culling to order a simple matter.

The siting of deer parks
By the beginning of the sixteenth century there were over forty parks in what is now Avon. They were to be found in most localities, with the exception of the low-lying levels and adjoining the Severn estuary. The greatest concentration was in the north of the county on the land released by the disafforestation of Kingswood. It was a well-wooded area, and made a good habitat for the fallow deer.

Early medieval parks were usually located beyond the areas of cultivated land, well away from manor houses and villages, often on the edge of a parish. They had fairly regular boundaries: either a circular or oval plan, or a rectangle with rounded corners (Fig. 3). A reasonable landlord would not sacrifice good farmland for a park, and parks were often located on low-quality land, such as steep slopes – as, for example, at Ashton Court, at Knole Park and Over Court at Almondsbury, Whitcliff Park outside Berkeley, and Sutton Court at Stowey Sutton.

Fig. 3. An aerial view of the former deer park at Hill Court, showing the curved boundary common to medieval deer parks.

Dyrham Park, however, only enclosed in 1510, was created close to the village and adjacent to the manor house, and as a result did involve the use of agricultural land. The licence allowed 500 acres/200 hectares of wood, pasture and meadow to be enclosed. Interestingly, a close examination of the present park (now half its original size) reveals extensive areas of ridge and furrow, testifying to the medieval agricultural use – the open fields having presumably been turned over to meadow and grazing some years before emparkment.

Parks are often associated with castles. Bristol Castle was a royal fortress which did not need its own park as it was so close to Kingswood Chase, which it administered. The park at Englishcombe was not far from Culverhay Castle. Some of the larger castles which continued to be inhabited through the Middle Ages were surrounded by a cluster of parks by the early sixteenth century. This was the case for both Thornbury, which had three large parks, and Berkeley, just over the county boundary in Gloucestershire. Berkeley's Whitcliff Park still has herds of deer, and, with its stone walls and keeper's lodge, retains the atmosphere of an exclusive preserve.

Some parks were 'unofficial', in that they were enclosed without royal licence. The deer park at Sutton Court is first recorded only in the 1530s but is likely to have existed before that, as it was owned by the St Loe family who managed several such unofficial parks.

The size of parks varied up and down the social scale. A lord with only one or two manors might have a park of only 100 acres/40 hectares, as was the case of the fourteenth-century park at Ubley, and there are plenty of references to parks of 30 acres/12 hectares or even less. However, some parks were much larger - the Duke of Buckingham's parks at Thornbury totalled more than 1,000 acres/400 hectares.

In addition to the royal forests, the King owned many royal parks, such as the one at Alveston; and the Bishop of Bath and Wells also had a large number of parks in the region – at Bath, Claverton, Banwell and Pucklechurch. Although the expense of maintaining a park was a major outlay for smaller landowners, major landlords could call on a considerable labour force to work in their parks. In the thirteenth century the Abbot of Glastonbury required each of his tenants in eleven manors, including Wrington, to do three days' work on his great park at Pilton in Somerset.

In 1507, the ostentatious Edward Stafford, Duke of Buckingham, began his grandiose scheme for making a palace of Thornbury Castle, which involved substantially increasing the size of the parks. Leland notes some thirty years later that one of the parks 'took in much faire ground very fruitful of corn . . . the inhabitants cursed the Duke for these lands so enclosed'. Evidently the curse worked; in 1521 Stafford was arrested and executed on a dubious charge of treason, and his lands were seized by the Crown. Archaeology has demonstrated that the extensions also involved the demolition of part of the hamlet of Kington on the west side of the park. Such devastating landscape changes were a notorious feature of later park-making, made famous by Goldsmith's poem 'The Deserted Village' (1770), but appear to have been rare in the medieval period.

Some medieval parks were, like landscape parks, uncompartmented, with grazing land dotted with pollards. Many others were divided into permanent compartments, and banks and ditches which remain today are indications of the divisions between coppice woods and 'launds' of open grazing.

Timber and grazing

Medieval parks had many functions in addition to supplying venison. They provided a useful supply of wood and timber, and grazing for local farmers. Timber trees for building were especially prized; in 1511, oaks from Marlwood Park were felled for the rebuilding at Thornbury Castle. Good quality building timber was much in demand, and supplies from parks were often transported considerable distances. Many grants of timber were made from Newton Park during the thirteenth century, usually to ecclesiastical buildings, one order being for seventy oaks. Newton Park also supplied high quality oak for carving, as was used for the choirstalls at Cleeve Abbey and for statuary at Glastonbury.

Fig. 4. Ancient oak pollards in Ashton Court – one of the finest collections in the south-west.

Wood for fires, hurdle-making, stakes and so forth was supplied by coppicing or pollarding, and some of the greatest trees in the county are ancient pollards. This form of management involved regular cropping of the branches at such a height that the regrowth was out of reach of deer and any other stock (Plate 3).

Coppicing was a similar process but carried out at ground level, which necessitated the enclosure of the area of newly coppiced wood to protect the regrowth. In the late thirteenth century, one fifth of Pen Park at Henbury was enclosed annually for the sale of such underwood. The coppice areas would also have contained trees allowed to grow up to full height for timber, while any trees in the launds would have been pollarded.

Grazing rights were often granted in paled areas of laund within the park. A sixteenth-century survey of Yate Park mentions 32 acres/13 hectares of meadow and pasture enclosed from the rest of the park.

One of the best collections of ancient wood-pasture pollards can be found, rather than easily seen, in Clerkencombe Wood at Ashton Court, where about two hundred oaks are still standing (Fig. 4). They would once have stood in the park, with deer grazing the grass between them, but changes in management ended the grazing, and recent growth of self-sown ash and sycamore has closed out the light and killed many of these magnificent living giants. Their fate illustrates how quickly abandoned parks can become woodland – often recorded in the common name Park Wood. Such trees are rare enough in the British Isles; they are even rarer in Europe as a whole. Britain holds a unique record for preserving old trees, and Bristol City Council must be congratulated on removing the new growth around the pollards at Ashton Court, and for its planned extension of the deer park into this area once again.

Rabbits and fish

Parks often enclosed warrens for the breeding and protection of hares and rabbits – the latter introduced by the Normans and needing, unlike today's, careful management. Mounds, now known as 'pillow-mounds', were constructed, with man-made burrows for the rabbits. A number survive: there are a couple in Yate Park where a sixteenth-century survey recorded a 'small warreyne for conyes', and there are other groups at Tortworth, Tormarton and Dyrham.

Fishponds, in which much-prized freshwater fish could be bred and produced for special feasts, were also often located within the security of a park. Medieval fishponds were functional in appearance, not dissimilar to a modern trout farm – a chain of ponds connected by a carefully managed flow of water, in which fish of different ages were fed and looked after (Fig. 5). They could be constructed either by damming a stream in a valley bottom, as was done at Over Park, or by constructing embanked ponds, as at Holm Park at Thornbury. Where parks were landscaped in the eighteenth century, such ponds often formed the basis of an ornamental lake or 'piece of water'.

Hunting lodges

Most early parks were at some distance from the house, and so a lodge was necessary, not only to house the park keeper but to shelter guests. Parks Farm at Chipping Sodbury stands in the centre of the former park, and still contains a

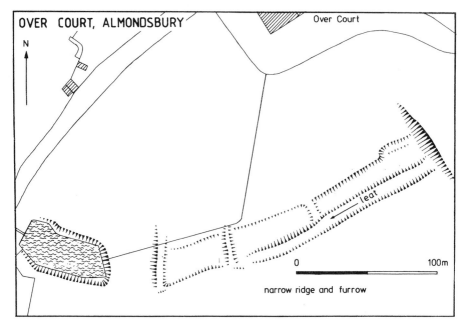

Fig. 5. A typical system of medieval fishponds, at Over Court, Almondsbury.

medieval wing which would have been the original lodge. When the park went out of use, in about 1600, it is recorded as having buildings already in it. Some lodges were moated. A well-preserved moat survives in a wood in what was formerly Hill Park. Yate Court, in the centre of what was Yate Park, still has a moat and would originally have been a lodge before the Berkeleys moved there in 1491 after being temporarily dispossessed of Berkeley Castle.

Surviving lodges can indicate the surprising extent of some medieval hunting grounds. Perhaps the most fascinating traces of extensive hunting grounds are those left by the Poyntz family of Acton Court. Apart from the main house, the family owned a network of subsidiary houses and hunting lodges, including the spectacular Newark Park at Wotton-under-Edge, and Tockington Lodge, recorded as a Poyntz residence in 1584. The deer park at Tockington, adjacent to the park of the royal manor of Alveston, was acquired by the Poyntz family in 1581. Remains of the lodge survive incorporated in the Tockington Park barn.

Poaching

The most frequent documentary reference to parks in medieval records is to the activities of poachers. Poachers were not always hungry or disaffected peasants; frequently, a manorial lord would poach or raid a neighbour's park. In 1523, William St Loe broke into Banwell Park with men armed with swords, bows, crossbows, nets and greyhounds. On that occasion he took more than twenty-four deer and added insult to injury by leaving their heads on the park palings. Some years later Sir William became the park keeper at Banwell. In the early sixteenth century several members of the Poyntz family of Acton Court raided the Bishop of Worcester's Pen Park at Henbury. A similar misdemeanour was committed by the Vicar of Dodington who, with several others, broke into Tormarton park and warren and took away deer, hares, rabbits and partridges.

The fate of early parks

Deer parks fell into disuse for a variety of reasons. As a wider range of food became more generally available in the sixteenth and seventeenth centuries, the prestige in owning significant herds of deer and other fresh food declined, and the role of parks became less important. Royal interest in hunting waned – although the unprecedented enthusiasm of Henry VIII and Elizabeth I for lavish ceremonial hunts did lead to a revival of park-making in Tudor times – while the unreasonable nature of Forest Law made its imposition increasingly impolitic; Henry VIII was the last to impose it with the reckless gusto of the Normans.

The commonest remaining evidence for a medieval deer park is the boundary bank and ditch – the ditch commonly on the inside. Fine examples survive at Alveston and Horton, and at Tormarton where the bank is over 5 feet/1.5 metres high. At Tockington, there are extensive remains of a great boundary bank and ditch – the bank 14 feet/4 metres wide in places (Fig. 6). At Yate Park, traces of a medieval wall enclosing the park can still be found, although far more spectacular are the ancient pollards – like those at Ashton Court or Eastwood Park.

Fig. 6. A characteristic surviving medieval deer park boundary and ditch at Tockington, near Almondsbury.

Early Gardens

Unlike parks, gardens are subject to continuous change. While the fabric – earthworks, excavations, stonework – may survive as archaeological remains, the planting of early gardens is known only from archival sources, or occasionally from soil analysis. From the medieval period onwards there are records of what plants were grown, and descriptions that indicate how highly pleasure gardens were regarded by those who could afford them.

Clear traces of gardens are revealed on old maps, and the science of garden archaeology has developed rapidly in the last ten years. Lumps and bumps are commonly left behind by the substantial earthworks involved in such early garden features as terraces, ramps, banks, parterres, ponds, canals and mounts; levels and crop marks seen from the air show us the layout of 'lost' gardens, and especially those of the sixteenth and seventeenth centuries.

Roman gardens

The earliest known garden remains in England derive from the villas of Roman settlers. Avon has one of the densest concentrations of Roman villas in the country, especially around Bath and in the Avon valley. Many have been excavated, but excavations in the earlier part of this century concentrated on the buildings. The larger examples of local villas are built around a central courtyard which almost certainly would have been a formal garden. These courtyards could be extremely large; one at the palatial villa at Keynsham measured 216 x 162 feet/65 x 50 metres Excavations elsewhere in the country, for example at Fishbourne in West Sussex, have revealed details such as ponds, fountains, box hedges and gravel paths. The Romans also introduced a number of trees which are now naturalised, such as the sweet chestnut and holm oak, as well as fruits such as cherry and fig.

These sophisticated classical gardens seem to have been abandoned when the Romans withdrew at the end of the fourth century, and there is no information on Anglo-Saxon gardens. We do know, however, that in King Alfred's time the Anglo-Saxon vocabulary included the names of many herbs and trees, revealing a considerable knowledge of botany, mainly for medicinal purposes.

Gardens from the Normans to the Tudors, 1066–1485

After the arrival of the Normans in 1066, evidence begins to emerge of gardens as we know them. In the Middle Ages (1066–1453), gardens would have been created around manor houses, castles and monasteries (Fig. 7). There was an important royal garden at Kingsholm outside Gloucester, and the pleasance of Llanthony Priory at Gloucester was, at the request of Queen Eleanor of Provence in 1277, linked by a bridge to the castle for the benefit of the royal guests; it had gardens, groves and an island with an elaborate *gloriet* or summerhouse, 'the Naight', on banks of the Severn.

Fig. 7. A fifteenth-century nobleman's pleasance, from the fifteenth-century Roman de la Rose.

Monastic gardens

Most abbeys and larger monasteries would have had several gardens and orchards. The accounts of Glastonbury Abbey, where the gardener in 1333–4 was Thomas of Keynsham, record the gardens comprising an orchard, a vineyard, a herb garden, vegetable plots, possibly some flower beds and some pasture. There is no mention of flowers but they may have been grown as a matter of course to decorate shrines and chapels. A hay crop and nettles were sold; cider and linen, onions, leeks and madder plants were also produced; and the garden yielded enormous quantities of garlic, valued for medicinal as well as for culinary purposes.

In Avon, there are two contrasting pieces of evidence concerning monastic gardens. The first is from the island of Steep Holm in the Bristol Channel. It was chosen as the site of a small monastery by Augustinian canons in the thirteenth century. They did not survive there long, but several of the flowers and herbs they introduced, such as the peony, still flourish on the island today.

The other example is the Carthusian priory at Hinton Charterhouse. The Carthusians were sometimes called 'the gardening monks' as a result of their unusual lifestyle. The monks lived in individual small houses around a communal cloister, and although they met in church and chapter house, they spent most of their time in solitude. They received basic provisions from the communal brewhouse and bakehouse, but relied for vegetables and herbs on their own gardens. The priory at Hinton has been excavated, revealing a large cloister surrounded by fifteen individual houses, each with its own L-shaped garden. When not reading, praying or working communally, the monks would occupy themselves by gardening, a devotional activity defined by the Book of Genesis.

Manor house gardens

The gardens of medieval manor houses did not differ greatly from monasteries, in that they too would be fairly small, and enclosed by a wall, hedge or even hurdles. They would have been predominantly functional, regular in layout, with straight paths and raised beds. Mid thirteenth-century records of the garden of the small manor house of Rimpton near Yeovil list produce that includes apples, pears, vines, flax, beans and peas.

Water was made into ornamental features in many gardens; many manorial fishponds lay adjacent to the house, and these functional elements were often combined with walks and planting for pleasure. There is a fine example of the remains of a chain of fishponds adjacent to the garden at Horton Court (Fig. 9), and another at the bishop's palace at Banwell. Moats would also have enclosed gardens as well as a house, as at Barr's Court moat at Kingswood. Some moats, such as those at Pucklechurch and Kenn Court, contained several subsidiary moats which appear to have enclosed small gardens and orchards reached by little bridges.

More elaborate gardens may have had lawns both for use as bowling greens and for aesthetic appeal. During the thirteenth and fourteenth centuries, gardens developed stylistically with the introduction of features such as tunnel arbours of wooden poles supporting climbing plants and vines, flowery meads, turf seats, pots of flowers, topiary and knots.

Gardens from Early Tudor Times to the Final Dissolution of the Monasteries, 1485–1540

Tudor gardens continued the tradition of the medieval *hortus conclusus*, forming a series of enclosures connected by covered walks. But with Henry VIII's royal gardens a new and grander layout was established – in conscious rivalry with François I and the French court, and influenced by the culture of the Italian Renaissance: a great garden designed to be looked down on from the state rooms. The basic design was a quartered square, with knot patterns and a central fountain. Three outstanding examples of this period are in Avon – at Thornbury Castle, Horton Court and Acton Court – and all three were built by men who had connections at the royal Court.

Thornbury Castle

The manor house at Thornbury was made into a 'castle' by Edward Stafford, 3rd Duke of Buckingham, who obtained a licence to castellate it in 1508 (Fig. 8). The castellations were part of a plan to create a palatial residence, but the scheme was abandoned when Buckingham was executed in 1521 and the castle passed to the Crown. However, a complex of gardens had already been laid out before his death.

Fig. 8. *Reconstruction of the early sixteenth-century Privy Garden at Thornbury, from Avray Tipping's* English Gardens *(1925).*

First, the 'Proper Gardeyn' or privy garden was made within the curtain wall and under the great oriel windows at Thornbury. Around the wall ran a 'gallerye of tymbre', as Leland noted in 1540, which would have overlooked a knot garden of some intricacy – Buckingham's gardener in 1520 was one John Wynde, rewarded for 'his diligence working and making knots'. A wooden cloister appears to have run across the whole walled enclosure, dividing the Proper Gardeyn from the western garden, which was also ornamented – the 1521 Crown Commissioners' Survey records 'a goodly gardeyn to walk ynne Closed wt high walls imbattled'. (The present mock-battlement yew hedging dates from the nineteenth century; yew was not planted in gardens until the seventeenth century.) Recent archaeological investigation by the Bath Archaeological Trust suggests that the sixteenth-century garden lies some 36 inches/90 centimetres below the present ground level. Outside the garden walls was a 'large and goodlye orcharde' of about 4 acres/1.5 hectares, 'walled about well and thick set with fruit trees of divers kinds of fruit'.

Horton Court

The garden remains at Horton Court are much smaller in scale than those at Thornbury. The Court was the home of William Knight, an ambassador for Henry VII and Henry VIII. He was educated at Ferrara University and made many trips to the continent, including visits to Rome in 1507 and 1527, negotiating Henry's

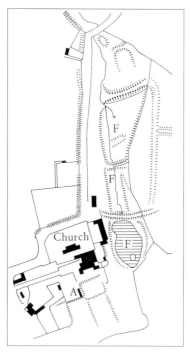

Fig. 9. Plan of garden remains at Horton Court, showing the terraces, chain of fishponds (marked F) and the ambulatory (marked A).

divorce from Catherine of Aragon. The house at Horton was built by 1521, and many of its features within display Knight's familiarity with Italian renaissance decoration. But in the garden is the most substantial Italianate feature, the 'ambulatory', an open loggia detached from the house (Plate 4). In Italy such a feature would allow for walking or sitting in the shade; here it was more likely to offer shelter from rain. Delicate columns support the arcade, and the back wall is decorated with medallions of classical figures. Below the ambulatory, linked to it by grass steps, a series of four terraces were laid out, descending towards the chain of medieval fishponds (Fig. 9). All this can still be seen, and makes Horton one of the most evocative gardens in the county.

Acton Court

The fortunes of the third garden, Acton Court, began to look up for the first time in three hundred years in the 1980s. Acton Court had been owned by the Keedwell family since World War I. They kept horses and ran riding stables, occupying only part of the house, which was smothered with ivy. Fierce dogs might greet a visitor rash enough to enter the yard, although one visitor who got on well with old Mr Keedwell was Edward VIII when he was Prince of Wales. But at Mr Keedwell junior's death in 1984, the estate was divided between his two sisters and put up for sale. A house of such antiquity, in such a decrepit state, propped up with

Fig. 10. Acton Court at the time of its rescue – a corner of the internal courtyard showing the junction of State Apartments and the Long Gallery.

Heath-Robinsonesque scaffolding and desperately vulnerable to unscrupulous development, brought Dorothy Brown of Bristol Visual and Environmental Group to the rescue (Fig. 10). The sixteenth-century Over Court at Almondsbury had been demolished in 1978, and the Trust feared that Acton Court might suffer a similar fate. It succeeded in buying the house at auction, and Acton Court subsequently became the first building taken into care by English Heritage.

There have since been tantalising investigations by Rob Iles and the Bath Archaeological Trust, under Rob Bell, which have revealed the extent of the historic garden. The line of the moat, of weirs, fishponds, canals, footings of bridges, garden walls, and the famous Kratzer sundial, form a fascinating but incomplete mosaic picture of an extensive and elaborate garden layout (Fig. 11).

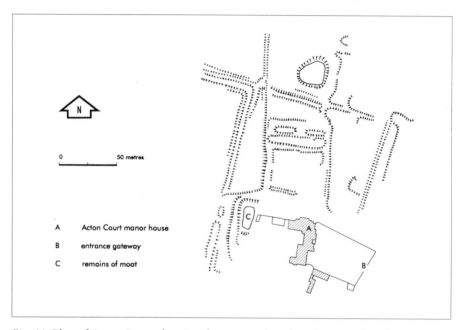

Fig. 11. Plan of Acton Court showing the extent of gardens discovered to date.

The builders of Acton Court, the Poyntz family, were not as powerful as their neighbour at Thornbury, but were nevertheless influential members of the Tudor Court. Acton Court was their principal residence, and has been identified by English Heritage as one of the three most important mid sixteenth-century houses in England. The present weird building – all rubble walls, rambling buttresses and seemingly random stone-mullioned windows – is only a fragment, the east end wing of the north range of a large courtyard mansion, probably built between 1530 and 1555 for Sir Nicholas Poyntz (Plate 5). Analysis of tree rings in the east wing's roof and floor beams shows they came from oaks felled in 1534-5, and we know that the range was specially built for the great visit of Henry VIII and Anne Boleyn in August 1535.

The key figure in the garden's history, however, was Nicholas's grandfather, Sir Robert Poyntz, who owned Acton Court from 1471 to 1520. He seems to have created the early sixteenth-century garden on the north side of the house. It was a walled enclosure of about 1 acre/0.4 hectare, separated from the house by a moat, across which two bridges connected with access from the house. As at Thornbury, there appears to have been a walk round the garden both at ground level and at first-floor level. To the north, on the garden's central axis, is a large circular pond, and another pond south of the moat also seems to have been part of an elaborate water garden and water supply system. Although this garden belonged to the earlier house, it was retained – perhaps not surprisingly, given its quality – and survived until the seventeenth century.

The elaborate sundial (Plate 6), dug up by chance during repair work to the foundations of the house, was identified by Sir George White as being designed by Nicholas Kratzer, horologist to Henry VIII. Initialled NK and dated 1520, it is the earliest surviving garden sundial in England. It is known that Henry VIII's gardens at Hampton Court featured a number of sundials, and it is tempting to wonder whether the courtier Poyntz copied any other features from those gardens. The scale of the emerging earthworks certainly indicates a very extensive complex at Acton Court.

Smaller manor house gardens

These three gardens were particularly elaborate, but many small manor houses had gardens based on such models. It is not always easy, without the detailed research described above, to disentangle features surviving from the early period from those of the Victorian revival. The basic structure of the garden of St Catherine's Court outside Bath, for example, may derive from the early sixteenth and early seventeenth centuries when the house was built and then extended (the balustrading is thought to be Jacobean), but much of the character of the garden is probably nineteenth-century, the house having been largely remodelled in a Victorian vision of the Tudor style (Fig. 53).

However, there appears to be no reason to doubt that the great walled bowling green at Little Sodbury Manor is the same one on which Henry VIII and Anne Boleyn witnessed a tournament during their royal progress in 1535. Acton Court may have provided the inspiration for Little Sodbury Manor, as John Walsh, who inherited the estate in the early sixteenth century, was a fellow courtier with Sir Robert Poyntz, and married Poyntz's daugher Ann. Leland records in 1542 that Walsh 'is Lord of Little Sodbyri, and hath a fayr place there in the syde of Sodbyri high hill and a park'. Most of the terracing, however, appears to date from the 1920s renovation of the house for Baron de Tuyll.

The gardens of these modest manor houses, like those of the grander establishments on which they were modelled, provide a foretaste of the explosion of grander formality in the seventeenth century.

Chapter 2

Dissolution to Enlightenment, 1540–1712

THE FINAL DISSOLUTION of the Monasteries, leading as it did to the spread of Protestant humanism, was a watershed in English cultural history – and garden history was no exception. It had a profound effect on land-ownership and land-use in the sixteenth century, as enormous tracts of land passed into new hands; major advances were made in fields such as the printing of books, resulting in the wide dispersal of horticultural knowledge; and accelerating competition with the Catholic countries over trade and exploration resulted in a whole new flora being revealed to the west.

Two Late Sixteenth-century Manor Gardens

There do not appear to have been any major new gardens created in the later sixteenth and early seventeenth centuries in what is now Avon. The best evidence for gardens of this period comes from those smaller sites, often manor houses, which were later abandoned by their owners. Good examples are Kelston Court and Claverton Manor, both near Bath and both abandoned in later centuries for a new house and park in a new location.

Kelston Court
Kelston Court was built between 1574 and 1589 by John Harrington and his son Sir John Harrington. Both men were courtiers, and Sir John achieved some notoriety for his book, *The Metamorphoses of Ajax* (1596), a satirical work on hydraulics which included a design for a privy (from which the word 'jakes' derived) and for other waterworks which he put into practice in the garden at Kelston. The manor house sited adjacent to the parish church was demolished in the mid eighteenth century when the present Kelston Park was built. What survives of the

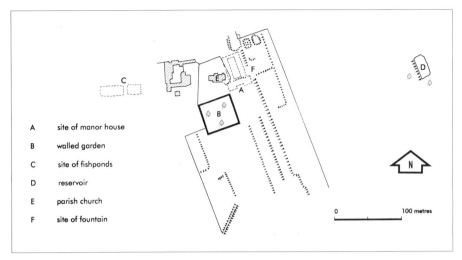

A   site of manor house

B   walled garden

C   site of fishponds

D   reservoir

E   parish church

F   site of fountain

Fig. 12. Plan of the garden remains at Kelston Court – the garden terraces and walks, and even the site of Harrington's famous fountain are still visible.

early garden is a series of scarps and low earthworks showing the position of terraces, walks and even flower beds (Fig. 12). A central feature of the garden was a fountain, forming part of a complex system of waterworks which also supplied the house. An eighteenth-century map appears to show an area of early parkland extending down to the site of the present mansion. The park had a number of straight double avenues, one of which led from the manor to a summerhouse over-looking the Avon valley (remembered today in the name Summerhouse Wood).

Claverton Manor
Claverton Manor is thought to have been built around 1580, and was demolished in about 1820 when, in the heyday of the reckless mania for prospects, the present Claverton House was built high on the slopes of the hill behind. But there are clear and spectacular remains of the old garden. The manor house had been built on a steep slope which was cut into five terraces, with the central platform occupied by the house. The lower terraces still have fine garden walls in pierced work, with steps connecting the different levels. Two of the garden walls have elaborate stone balustrades (Fig. 13)

Prospects and Private Beauties – Restoration gardens and the Dutch style

During the latter part of the seventeenth century, gardens and parks remained geometrical in layout, but became far more elaborate and extensive. Although gardens were still divided from the park by a physical barrier such as a wall, the grand manner imported from France after the Restoration meant extending the design, and evidence of ownership, out into the surrounding landscape, often capitalising on a distant feature such as a church tower. Viewing terraces or raised

Fig. 13. The terraced gardens at Claverton Manor in a zincograph of c.1840.

walks enabled the visitor to enjoy prospects of the park or countryside beyond the garden wall.

While avenues and prospects stretched away to the horizon, within the garden there were extraordinary variations on the old formal themes: knots were metamorphosed into *parterres de broderie*, with filigree patterned beds; topiary reached new heights of absurdity savagely ridiculed by Pope ('A Pair of Giants, stunted . . . A Lavender Pig with Sage growing in his Belly'); while water became ever more elaborately employed.

It is interesting how often landscape prospects featured in seventeenth-century layouts. As topographical artists show, these gardens were not as inward-looking as is often claimed. For half the county of Avon, the detailed topographical views of Johannes Kip (produced for Robert Atkyns's *Ancient and Present State of Glostershire* (1712), but probably dating from the preceding decade) provide us with a unique record of gardens at this time.

Kingsweston – *'delightful gardens and a full prospect'*
At Kingsweston (or King's Weston) outside Bristol, for example, Kip records an elaborate formal layout around a late sixteenth-century house (Fig. 14). Sir Robert

Southwell had bought the estate in 1679, and the gardens seem to have been laid out under his direction. They included a fine large parterre, a wilderness to the south-east of the house, and an orangery. The fine brick-built banqueting house behind Vanbrugh's loggia would have given views over the road and towards the Severn. In the park, dramatic avenues stretched out to Penpole Point where there was a viewing tower. In 1712, Atkyns wrote that Southwell 'hath a pleasant seat with delightful gardens, and a full prospect over Kingsweston road, the harbour of the City of Bristol and over the Severn Sea into Wales'.

The present house, designed for Southwell by Sir John Vanbrugh, was built between 1710 and 1725, together with a number of garden buildings: the Echo, Penpole Gate, the Brewhouse and the Loggia. Apart from the Brewhouse, they all replaced earlier buildings shown by Kip (Fig. 14). But few alterations were made

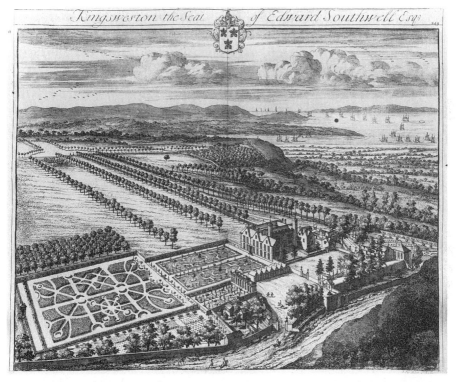

Fig. 14. Kip's view of Kingsweston from Robert Atkyns's The Ancient and Present State of Glostershire *(1712).*

to the gardens, and the new house was slotted into the old surroundings. The result was much admired, despite Vanbrugh's waning star. The Reverend Jeremiah Milles thought it a very fine house, and particularly admired the Loggia ('a very beautifull summer house'), but his real rapture was for the 'glorious prospect of ye Bristol Channel'. This great baroque layout was overlaid by the informal landscaping of the later eighteenth century (though the buildings remained), but recent survey work and restoration proposals suggest that it could be recovered.

Sneyd Park
The most astonishing evidence of the taste for prospects is the enormous curved terrace that Kip shows stretching down from the mid seventeenth-century house at Sneyd Park to an eminence above the River Avon (Fig. 15). Despite the fashion for views, this gigantic terrace must still have been a phenomenon at the time, and its existence is witnessed by the first Ordnance Survey map *c*.1882. It took the visitor out into unimproved countryside, with a panorama of the river and its traffic as its culminating glory.

The house, owned by the Jackson family, stood on elevated ground, with a parterre and kitchen gardens lying alongside each other in typical seventeenth-century style. Later in the century Celia Fiennes, on her tours, was always admiring flowers and eating fruit in the same step; as she strolled round she would pick 'apricock, peach, plumb and necktarine', noting 'dwarfe trees of fruit and flowers and greenes [evergreens] in all shapes, intermixt with beds of strawberyes for ornmanent and use'. In 1693 the house was let to John Cook, Chamberlain of

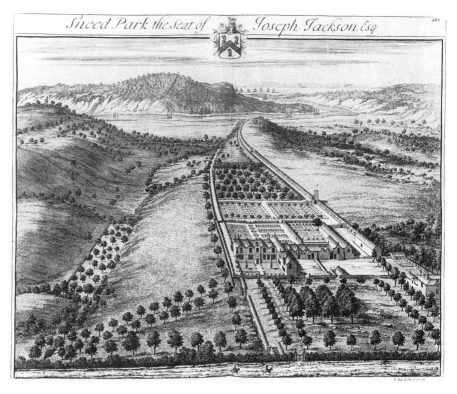

Sneed Park the Seat of Joseph Jackson Esq

Fig. 15. *Kip's view of Sneyd Park showing the extraordinary viewing terrace curving down to the Avon.*

Bristol, and he built the octagonal tower which – as Cook's Folly – features in so many eighteenth- and nineteenth-century picturesque views of the Avon. The tower was demolished in 1932, and Sneyd Park itself was pulled down in the mid twentieth century.

Dodington – a romantic situation
Little survives of the early gardens that predated the landscaping of the eighteenth century at Dodington, but they are evocatively described by Alexander Pope, who visited in 1728. He described the house as 'pretty enough, the situation romantic, covered with woody hills stumbling upon one another confusedly, and the garden makes a valley between them with some mounts and waterfalls'. Pope's interest is clearly as much in the surrounding landscape as in the garden.

Dyrham – 'curious waterworks . . . beautiful Irregularity'
At Dyrham, below the statue of Neptune, now without his kingdom, a prodigious water garden was built for William Blathwayt between about 1691 and 1704, with advice from George London, the leading designer of the day (Fig. 16). Blathwayt was Secretary of State to William III, and the gardens at Dyrham reflect the Dutch

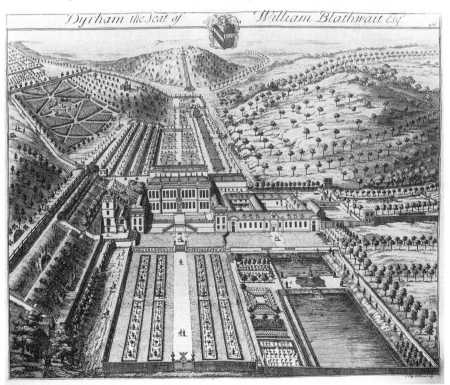

Fig. 16. Kip's view of Dyrham. Despite the apparently impossible extravagance of his depiction, Kip's accuracy is borne out by other sources.

taste that was *de rigueur* in royal circles – not the domestic Dutch style of topiary hedges and tulipomania, but the grandeur of William's palace at Het Loo. Kip shows a cascade running down the hillside into a long canal that stretched to the orangery and was lined with bay, orange and lemon trees in pots during the summer months. In front of the house was a parterre in quarters, and on the bank to the north, above a series of six ascending terraces decorated with statues, fountains, fruit trees and seats, an elaborate wilderness. This was by no means wild, but was a geometrically divided shrubbery with straight walks, a central garden, statues, and even covered seats with lecterns for outdoor reading (Fig. 17).

Fig. 17. The Wilderness at Dyrham. With its little outdoor reading desks Stephen Switzer thought it the place for 'the sublimest studies'.

Throughout the wilderness the walks commanded views out – to the church and into the garden below, or out of the whole domain to the surrounding countryside. In 1718, Stephen Switzer admired the layout's 'beautiful Irregularity' – which, given its geometric form, gives us some idea of the straitjacket which Switzer felt had dominated garden design up to this time. The intricate garden was complemented by those outward views, and by features such as the curving chestnut walks out into the park. The Kip engraving is a picture to pore over and lose yourself in, and its accuracy is borne out by Switzer's description.

The purchases of seeds and plants by Blathwayt are well documented, with many bills to suppliers (Fig. 18). From Virginia he obtained the latest exotics – tulip trees, sassafras and Virginia pine – while George London supplied Blathwayt's head gardener, Thomas Hurnall, with seeds from one of his other substantial local

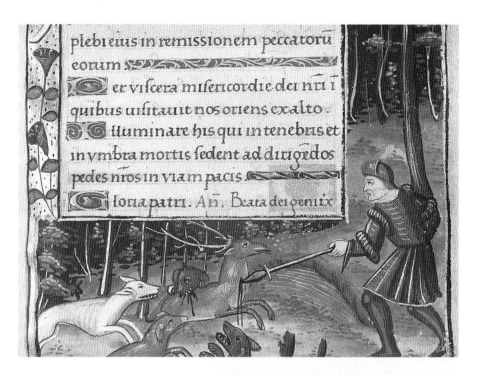

Plate 1 (above). A deer hunt, from a fifteenth-century illuminated manuscript.
Plate 2 (right). Fallow deer in the park at Ashton Court.

Plate 3. One of the oldest oak pollards in the county, in Eastwood Park at Falfield.

Plate 4. The garden at Horton Court, with William Knight's classical ambulatory.

Plate 5. Acton Court from the east – its grandeur still evident despite the fallow years since the Poyntzes' time.

Plate 6. The Kratzer sundial which would have been a feature in the gardens of Acton Court. Sundials are known to have ornamented the gardens of Henry VIII at Hampton Court.

Plate 7. A page from the Duchess of Beaufort's 'Florilegium', or flower book, painted by Everard Kickius. The index describes the central flower, a borage, as Cynoglossum maximum montanum or belgicum; to the right is a polyanthus and to the left an auricula with unusual variegated leaves.

Plate 8 (above). Thomas Robins's painting of Henbury, c.1758, showing the early layout in its rural setting.

Plate 9. William Kent's Worcester Lodge at Badminton.

Plate 10. Stoke Park in its landscape setting, seen from Purdown.

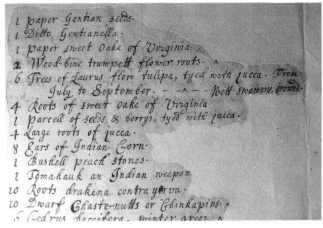

Fig. 18. An inventory of goods for Dyrham shipped from Virginia on board 'The Jeffery' in a chest and a barrel. The list includes roots, seeds, berries, trees and other plants.

commissions, Longleat in Wiltshire.

The Dyrham garden was extravagant to build and costly to maintain. A survey of 1766 records the gardens much as they appear in Kip, but in 1769 'the curious waterworks' were said by Rudder in his county history to be 'much neglected and going to decay', and by 1791 the gardens were gone, 'reconciled to modern Taste', with Neptune more like Robinson Crusoe left surveying the deserted scene.

Smaller gardens – Tortworth, Wick and Siston

Not all garden layouts were such prodigies as that at Dyrham. The garden recorded by Kip at sixteenth-century Tortworth Court was clearly extended piecemeal as gardening fashions developed, without remodelling earlier parts (Fig. 19). Thus there are kitchen gardens close to the house on the north, located within what looks like part of a medieval moat, which are likely to date from the building of the house. To the east, what appears to be former fishponds have been incorporated in a later formal garden with raised tree-lined walks connected to the house by a large sunken lawn. Then, almost incongruously, an elaborate French-style *parterre de broderie* is recorded on the land south of the church – laid out, judging by its style, in the 1660s to 1680s.

We can thank that unpretentious continuity for the survival of the Tortworth (sweet) Chestnut, which would have been ancient when the house was built. It was retained even when a formal parterre garden was laid out immediately to the east of it – the proximity necessary in order that the garden should align on the house. The tree can be seen on the Kip looming most ungeometrically over the garden. The house was abandoned when the new Tortworth Court was built in 1849–50, and apart from the chestnut, only evocative grassy lumps and bumps survive of the garden.

A similarly modest layout was recorded by Kip at Wick Court, where the house of *c*.1620–30 is shown surrounded by fine walled enclosures, parterres and orchards

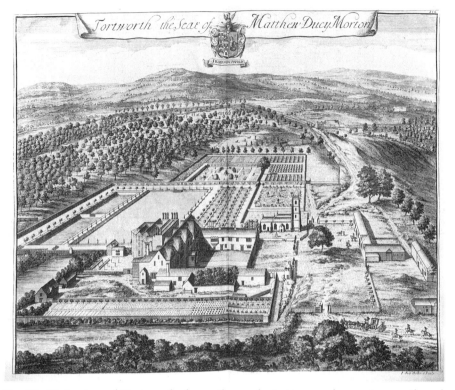

Fig. 19. Kip's view of Tortworth shows the garden's piecemeal organic growth and development.

(Fig. 20). Old yews survive to this day, as do remains of a sunken parterre, a summerhouse and a walled kitchen garden.

Siston Court seems to have been built between 1572 and 1598 by Sir Richard Denys. By 1712, there were extensive geometrical gardens which Kip recorded in his engraving.

Tulipomania and the Cult of Flora

The sixteenth century saw a great increase in foreign trade, especially with the Ottoman empire, and this introduced the west to a new garden flora of trees, shrubs and herbaceous plants. Dr John Harvey has shown the enormous range of new species that arrived in this period – anemone, hyacinth, narcissus, ranunculus and tulip; cherry laurel, laurustinus, lilac and syringa; yellow jasmine, various species of iris and lily and the Crown Imperial, together with bulbs such as spring crocus. Nurseries sprang up to retail these new imports, and their catalogues afford a unique record for gardeners with an interest in historical planting.

By the 1630s the idea of 'florists' flowers' had emerged – flowers grown purely for beauty without any herbal value, the results of experiments in hybridisation,

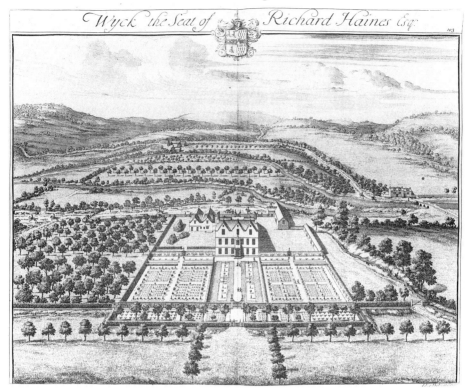

Fig. 20. Wick Court by Kip – some of the yews survive to this day.

and particularly favoured by collectors. The first botanic garden in England was opened in 1621 in Oxford, and hybridisation developed rapidly. In the Netherlands in the 1630s, the craze for ever more elaborate tulip cultivars led to 'tulipomania' – when bulbs changed hands for vast sums, and speculators were often left bankrupt by the gambling involved. The first tulip bulbs had only arrived in Europe from Turkey in the 1550s. By the mid seventeenth century 'florists' flowers' included the carnation, ranunculus, tulip and amenone; to be joined later by the auricula, hyacinth, polyanthus and pink.

A patroness of Botany
One of the leading lights in the florists' world was Mary, 1st Duchess of Beaufort. In the sheltered formal gardens at Badminton she cultivated many of the newly introduced exotics from as far afield as southern Africa. She was also a notable patron, 'much celebrated throughout Europe for promoting natural learning': her protégé, Richard Bradley, who went on a buying trip to the Netherlands for her, became, despite his lack of formal training, Professor of Botany at Cambridge. Her brother was an eminent horticulturalist – his gardens at Cassiobury were admired by John Evelyn – and the Duchess corresponded and swapped flowers with the foremost gardeners such as the Bobarts, father and son, at the Oxford Botanic

Garden, and Sir Hans Sloane of the Chelsea Physic Garden. Respect for her as 'a patroness of Botany' was strong, and the genus Beaufortia, brought back from Australia by Captain Cook in 1787, was named in her honour.

Best of all, when she was over seventy, the Duchess commissioned a Florilegium, a painted record of her flowers, from the Dutch painter Everard Kickius. His vivid and detailed paintings, painted on vellum between 1703 and 1705, provide a unique record of these early cultivars (Plate 7). After the first volume was finished, a Badminton footman, Daniel Frankcom, also revealed a talent for flower-painting, and a second volume was completed.

Town gardens

Many of the foremost florists were town-dwellers. Early maps, such as Hoefnagel's of Bristol in 1581 and Smith's of Bath from 1588, had shown the extent of private gardens within the old city boundaries at that time. Millerd's map of Bristol in *c*.1671 and Gilmore's of Bath in *c*.1692 provide further fascinating records of the two cities, this time on the eve of their great expansion in the eighteenth century. Gilmore's in particular shows gardens in some detail (Fig. 21).

In Walcot Street the gardens ran right down to the river, with as yet very little back land development. A contemporary painting of the garden at Ladymead House, a little further up-river, gives us some idea of the appearance of these town sites, although this one was larger and probably more elaborate than most. It was strictly formal. The house stood on a terrace overlooking the sloping garden, and on the main axis of the house lay an area of rectangular lawns and walks, apparently of gravel, ornamented with clipped bushes and four ornate topiary features. The only plants which were allowed to grow naturally appear to have been the climbers on the walls of the house. A canal divided this area from the more utilitarion section containing four large rectangular enclosures, presumed to have been used for fruit and vegetable growing. Along the river there was a tree-lined walk, terminated at one end by a summerhouse and at the other by an alcove seat, while a gate gave access to the river bank.

We do not know much about the plants that grew in the Ladymead garden, but an attempt to recreate the authentic planting of a late sixteenth- or early seventeenth-century garden has been made at the Red Lodge in Bristol (Fig. 22).

The garden today is only a fragment of the layout that stretched from the lodge down to John Younge's Great House which stood on the site of the Colston Hall. The estate was split up after Younge's death, soon after the lodge was built *c*.1590, but the garden survived intact until the 1780s when most of it was sold for building, leaving only the 77-foot/22-metre square below the Red Lodge. In 1742 John Rocque had recorded the gardens, in his survey of Bristol, as descending in three terraces to Trenchard Street behind the original house. The more elaborate gardens were naturally those closest to the house.

Today, the orientation of the recreated garden has changed, and the little formal garden lies under the windows of the main rooms of the Lodge. Bristol City Council

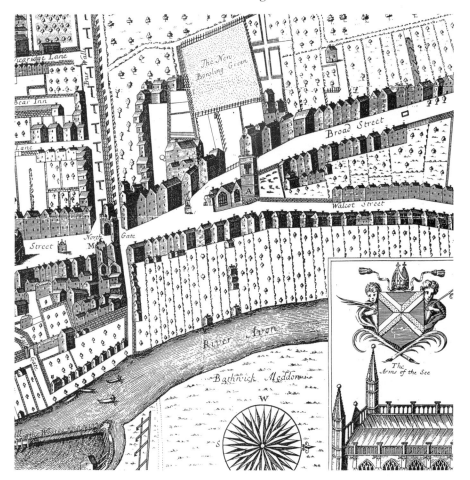

Fig. 21. A detail of Joseph Gilmore's map of Bath, c.1692, showing the private gardens in Walcot Street.

has used a knot pattern taken from one of the plaster ceilings, and plants from the period 1590 to 1630. This just allows dwarf box as an edging plant for the main knot (the hyssop and germander which edge the outer beds are more likely to have been used in the 1590s), while the outer beds are filled with flowers, shrubs and herbs taken from Gerard's *Herball* of 1597, with advice from John Harvey of the Garden History Society. The trellis screening some of the surrounding twentieth-century buildings is taken from a French work, *Maison Rustique*, translated into English in 1600.

The walls of seventeenth-century town gardens are generally peppered with small holes left from the nails to which trees were tied and trained in espaliers and fans ('nail'd neate', as Celia Fiennes remarked), and sheltered gardens such as the Red Lodge and Ladymead would have offered an ideal environment for some of the tender fruit she mentions. A fine display of seventeenth-century-style fruit

Fig. 22. Red Lodge garden, Bristol, recreated using authentic planting from the period 1590–1630.

growing can be seen further up the Severn at Westbury Court where the National Trust has restored the Dutch-style water garden and planted it with great authenticity, using the remarkably detailed plant lists that survive from the late seventeenth century.

Public Walks

As Bath and Bristol developed in the seventeenth and early eighteenth centuries, the demand for recreational areas grew. When Celia Fiennes visited Bath in about 1687 there were only two 'places for divertion'. There was 'the Kings Mead, which is a pleasant green meaddow, where are walkes round and cross it, no place for coaches'; she added that it had 'severall little Cakehouses where you have fruit Sulibubs and sumer liquours to entertain the Company that walke there'. The other place was 'the Gravel Walks', which John Wood described in his *Essay towards a*

Description of Bath of 1742–3:

> On the South Side . . . there is a paved walk of two hundred feet in length and twenty seven feet in Breadth, which, not many years ago, was the only place of general resort in the City for Pleasure and Exercise . . .

The walks comprised the central paved alley for 'the company' (that is, those in Bath for the spas), and two other gravelled alleys outside, 'for the common Sort of People'. But the development of Bath in the first years of the eighteenth century saw increased provision: Harrison's Assembly Rooms of 1708 included Harrison's Walks beside the river, which became very popular 'and were looked upon as prejudicial to the Gravel Walks', by now also known as 'the Grove'. In response, the Corporation took down the sycamores in 1732, and remodelled the whole as the Orange Grove after an opportune visit by the Prince of Orange in 1734, to whom the central obelisk was dedicated (Fig. 23).

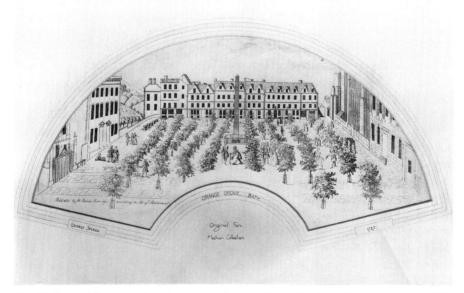

Fig. 23. Printed fan, showing view in the Orange Grove, Bath, by George Sperren, 1737. The walks were still as formal as they had been in Celia Fiennes's time.

In Bristol, there was even less provision of public open space. Apart from College Green, there was only the Marsh – now occupied by Prince Street and Queen Square – which had long been laid out for walks and recreation (Plate 15); Tyson records in his *Memorials of Queen Square* (1843) that in 1610, when the Duke of Brunswick came to Bristol, 'the Mayor with some of the magistrates gave his Grace a walk about the Marsh to show him some pleasure'. Apart from shady walks, the Marsh also afforded space for entertainments such as bear-baiting and firework displays. From 1699, however, the City began letting it out in plots for building a grandiose and modern development centred on Queen Square.

Parks – the Decline of Deer and the Rise of Avenues

Few medieval parks in Avon have continued in unbroken use as deer parks. Some were adapted as landscape parks; many were actually disparked and turned back into farmland, particularly in the seventeenth century – a simple matter, if the deer had been allowed to destroy the trees. The park at Sutton Court is described in the 1630s as 'newly enclosed', that is divided up with quickthorn hedges, after the lord of the manor sold the land to his tenant.

In the 1530s, John Leland reported of the park belonging to the Priory of Bath on Combe Down that the walls were derelict and the park empty of deer – a result perhaps of the economic and social pressure on the clergy during the latter part of Henry VIII's reign. A grange was recorded as being located on the south-east margin of the fishponds at the bottom of the slope, which also had 'vineyards and gardens and shady groves'. For two hundred years after Leland's visit the park remained in purely agricultural use before it was acquired by Ralph Allen.

The post-medieval period saw many parks dismantled, but others were given a new lease of life. Ashton Court, first emparked in 1392, was revived when it came into the hands of the Smyth family in the ·mid sixteenth century, as was Badminton when it was taken over by the earls of Worcester in the mid seventeenth century. The new owners greatly extended these parks over succeeding generations, and both contain deer to this day.

In the latter part of the seventeenth century, influenced by Charles II's enthusiasm for the French grand manner, houses were often complemented by elaborate layouts of avenues. Many of these magnificent and ostentatious features have disappeared, but some have survived – remnants of the avenue at Henbury survived until the 1960s, untouched by the 'judicious axe' of Humphry Repton.

The most extensive layout of avenues in the county was at Badminton. Here a great house was built for, and possibly to the designs of, the 1st Duke of Beaufort between 1664 and 1691. The Duke, who rose to power through support for Cromwell, successfully transferred allegiance to Charles II and the Stewart cause against William of Orange, and then, amazingly and with equal success, transferred allegiance to William.

Kip's four engravings of the house and its estate show the immense radiating and cross avenues (Fig. 24). The impression of boundless property was partly illusory – Roger North records that the neighbouring landowners planted continuations of the Duke's avenues 'to humour his vistos' – but the resulting effect is still a staggering impression of power. Celia Fiennes wrote of the view from the leads (the only place from where the illusion can be enjoyed to the full) that from there you could 'look 12 ways down to the parishes and grounds beyond all thro' glides or vistos of trees; the Gardens', she adds, 'are very fine and Water works'. The effect is brilliantly conveyed in the slightly dizzy perspectives of Kip, and in the fine paintings of Thomas Smith of about 1700. The avenues, although blurred by later infill planting and reduced in extent, still dominate the Badminton scene, the Centre Walk Avenue extending south-east beyond the M4 and past Littleton Drew.

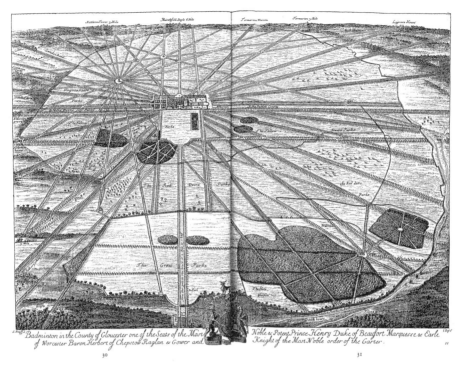

Fig. 24. Kip's dizzying bird's-eye view of the avenues at Badminton.

Another dramatic late seventeenth-century avenue layout was at Henbury (see Plate 8). Here, a double avenue led from the great house of Sir Samuel Astry straight to the top of Blaise Hill, albeit at a slightly skewed angle. The hill appears to have been ornamented with concentric or spiral walks, and a summerhouse was built on the summit, on the supposed site of the chapel of St Blaise. This point afforded magnificent views of the surrounding countryside and sea.

A system of avenues was laid out at Newton Park, probably during the late seventeenth century, around the old fourteenth-century fortified manor house. The avenues seem to have been laid out after Joseph Langton bought the estate in 1666, and before Capability Brown was consulted in 1761, although Brown evidently retained much of the layout, as is shown in the 1789 survey (Plate 23). A few elms survived from this layout until the 1970s, and have been replaced by Norway maple. It was a surprising characteristic of the landscape revolution described in the next chapter that it by no means turned its back on the past.

Chapter 3

The Eighteenth Century

THE EARLY EIGHTEENTH CENTURY, the period of Enlightenment, saw great changes in people's concept of Nature and its role in parks and gardens. Debates on Nature, together with other influences such as the taste for Italian landscape painting engendered by the Grand Tour, resulted in the emergence of the distinctively English idea of 'landscape gardening'. After the social and political upheavals of the seventeenth century, the eighteenth was a period of relative stability and order in England, when many landowners had the time and money to create expansive parks around their country seats. Around Bristol especially, new industrial wealth brought a vast injection of cash into estates.

Vast areas of land were involved: 850 acres/340 hectares at Ashton Court, 600 acres/240 hectares around Dodington, 325 acres/130 hectares at Blaise. Thousands of young saplings were planted; if necessary, tons of earth were moved to 'improve' the natural contours. This sort of landscaping was only possible in a society which concentrated huge wealth in the hands of a few families, in which labour was cheap, and where continuity in land-ownership from generation to generation was assured. The great landscape gardens of the eighteenth century, refashioning or moulding the existing landscape, incorporating here, discarding there, took decades to create.

The debate over Nature versus Art was led principally by the 3rd Earl of Shaftesbury and Joseph Addison. In his *The Moralists, a philosophical rhapsody,* of 1709, Shaftesbury developed the notion of 'enthusiasm' and communion with 'GLORIOUS Nature! supremely Fair, and sovereignly Good! All-loving and All-lovely, All-divine!' In more measured terms, Addison praised the 'beautiful Wildness of Nature' in his highly regarded *Spectator* essays of 1712. Addison actually addressed himself to landowners, exhorting them, 'Why may not a whole

Estate be thrown into a kind of Garden . . . ? A Man might make a pretty Landskip of his own Possessions' – and the notion of 'the luxury of Nature' being preferable to 'nice Art' began to take hold.

Alexander Pope and 'the simplicity of the ancients'

Despite the rhetoric, however, the first gardens laid out under this influence did not look like a park by Brown, nor like a painting by Claude. Alexander Pope, admired both for his garden and for his poetry, was the most immediately influential advocate of the new style, in which he invoked what he called the 'simplicity of the ancients':

> In all, let Nature never be forgot
> But treat the Goddess like a modest fair,
> Nor over-dress, nor leave her wholly bare.

The ideal, expressed here in the 'Epistle to Burlington', drew on Horace's metaphor of the youth who neither left his hair unkempt nor decorated it with ornaments, but simply braided it. Pope is far from suggesting the banishment of apparent Art – for which Brown would later be admired. His was a style which would still strike us as highly artificial (green amphitheatres, wilderness groves, colonnades, terraces, mounts, subterranean grottoes and quincunxes) but which aimed to avoid subjugating natural irregularity to rule and line. Pope's most famous advice was to 'consult the Genius of the Place' – to respond to the evocative qualities of an individual site rather than lay out a garden to a predetermined formula.

Pope at Prior Park – the 'next-to-natural'

When Ralph Allen, so influential in the development of Bath, had his prodigious mansion built in the 1730s – a gigantic billboard advertising the virtues of his Bath stone – Pope helped him design a suitable garden. Pope visited regularly, as well as offering regular advice and encouragement in letters between 1736 and 1743. He appears from the correspondence to have been involved in laying out walks through the woods and opening views from them, in the planting of new trees, and in designing Mrs Allen's grotto and cascade. Richard Graves also attributes the design of the Sham Bridge in the Wilderness to Pope.

The description of Prior Park in Samuel Richardson's 1742 version of Defoe's *Tour* is a perfect mirror of Pope's ideals as set out in the 'Epistle to Burlington'. Allen, he writes,

> pursues only what the natural Scite points out to him . . . He levels no Hills,
> but enjoys the Beauty of the Prospects they afford; he cuts down no Woods,
> but strikes thro' them fine Walks and next-to-natural Mazes; and has, but
> that Means, a delightful Grove always filled with Birds, which afford the
> Rural Ear a Musick transcending all others.

The recent historic landscape survey for the National Trust by Land Use Consultants has drawn particular attention to this early layout at Prior Park. Land Use Consultants suggest it comprised a central narrowing vista, leading from the

Fig. 25. Anthony Walker's engraving of Prior Park in 1752, showing the semi-formal layout inspired by Pope.

house down to a circular pool about half way down the present slope, between hedges punctuated by urns; with, to the right, a grove, to the left the wilderness where twisting curving paths led through the woodland, enlivened by regularly serpentine rills and features such as the grotto, a statue of Moses, and a circular 'room' in the middle. The whole terminated at the bottom with a retaining wall. In 1746, Charles Yorke wrote admiringly of the layout as having balanced 'Wilderness and cultivation . . . without adding anything from art' – according to the Horatian ideal.

Widcombe Manor – not overdressed nor wholly bare

The history of the garden at Widcombe Manor is not clear, but the house was remodelled in about 1727 for Philip Bennet, and field evidence indicates that a fine garden was laid out at the same time. This comprised two broad terraces below the house, at the end of one of which the classical summerhouse survives, designed possibly by Richard Jones, clerk of works to Ralph Allen at Prior Park. The terraces overlooked what appears to have been a tiny park with, on the far side, a formal pool, a cascade and a 30-foot/9-metre high viewing mound, on top of which two enormous eighteenth-century yews are still growing. A beautifully preserved spiral path ascends to the viewing platform. With the formal features around the pastoral dell, this is a fine example of the artful and natural in balance, as advocated by Pope. Later developments, most notably Harold Peto's work on the terraces in the early twentieth century, have not detracted from this rare survival.

The 'artinatural' style

The principles that lay behind Pope's style differed from those that animated the more intensely ornamented gardens that are sometimes termed rococo in recognition of their mannered, curvilinear, asymmetric style; Batty Langley, who took the style to extremes, called it the 'artinatural'. These intricate and often quite small-scale gardens have been vulnerable to changes of management or taste, and very few survive. The best local example is at Painswick in Gloucestershire, where the Rococo Garden is being restored, using Thomas Robins's view of 1748.

Of course, not all owners were in the vanguard of fashion, especially in remote Somerset and Gloucestershire. A wealthy Bristol merchant, Abraham Elton, bought the medieval manor house of Clevedon Court in 1708 (Fig. 26). Over the next ten

Fig. 26. Clevedon Court as depicted in an anonymous oil painting, 1721.

years or so, he laid out terraces on the two ancient fortified fosseways that ran along the side of Court Hill above the house, built a summerhouse on the summit of the hill, clothed the hill with plantations of trees, and planted avenues running across the hill towards Bristol and Clevedon. Two great trees, a lime and a horse chestnut, survive from these at the foot of the hill. This was a conservative and respectable layout designed, as Margaret Elton has observed, to proclaim that 'brocaded tradesmen' or merchants were now gentlemen. And elsewhere, owners retained unfashionable features such as avenues throughout this period of change – as we see, for example, in the post-Brown survey of Newton Park.

Fermes Ornées

One response to Addison's suggestion that 'a man might make a pretty Landskip of his own Possessions' was the ornamentation of farmland as a *ferme ornée*.

Stephen Switzer was also advocating such ornamentation, and famous examples were laid out at Woburn Farm in Surrey, *c*.1738 onwards, and at the Leasowes in Warwickshire from 1745. But these were fragile decorations laid out on peripheral land, and reduced management quickly resulted in their decay. An interesting late example of a *ferme ornée* (from the 1780s) is Folly Farm at Stowey Sutton, now managed by the Wildlife Trust. Here, streams were ornamented with walks and bridges over cascades and pools, clumps were planted on viewpoints, and a walk conducted the visitor round a succession of different areas. Intriguingly, there appears to have been cooperation and shared views with the neighbouring Stowey estate, where in 1793 a survey made recommendations for enhancing the landscape and adding 'Ornament and profit to the Estate'.

William Kent – tasting the charms of landscape

The greatest of the early landscape designers was William Kent, of whom Horace Walpole wrote: 'painter enough to taste the charms of landscape . . . he leaped the fence, and saw that all nature was a garden'. The key discovery, or rediscovery, for it was first used by the much despised French formal gardeners, was the ha-ha or invisible fence, made by a ditch rather than a hedge or wall, which allowed views out from the garden. Avenues were anathematised, and the symmetry of seventeenth-century gardens shown by Kip was deplored.

Kent's only work in Avon was at Badminton in 1745, late in his life, where he encouraged the removal of the formal gardens and the construction of the lake. His impact on the great formal layout at Badminton was only partial, his main contribution being the design for Worcester Lodge (Plate 9). It had a double function as both a destination for rides from the house (the dining room over the archway is one of Kent's best interiors) and as a Palladian exclamation mark at the beginning of the great approach to the house. It is a great building but, standing ironically at the head of one of the grandest avenues in the country, hardly illustrates Kent's contribution to landscape gardening.

The Wizard of Durham

Another genius of the pre-Brownian era, however, left a more notable mark on Avon. Thomas Wright, astronomer, gardener, architect, antiquary, mathematician and occasional drawing master to the aristocracy, worked on three sites in Avon. People called him the 'Wizard of Durham', and his designs suggest a bizarre and wonderful imagination.

He designed a layout for the east front of Badminton, which was an extraordinary vision of serpentising paths, shrubberies, flower gardens, temples in the Gothick and Chinese taste, a 'magical' mathematical grove, arbours and menagerie. Inevitably, perhaps, it was never implemented, but a 'ruined' Ragged Castle, which served as a dwelling until after World War II, a number of other lodges, the great eyecatcher Castle Barn, and the root house in the park were all constructed to his designs. Root houses were popular garden ornaments in the eighteenth and early nineteenth centuries. Built of branches and roots – the more grotesquely twisted the better – lath and plaster, they were ephemeral by nature and rarely survive (this one is listed Grade I for that reason). The building epitomises the ironic pastoral whimsy of the pre-Brownian style, blending rustic crudeness with rococo delicacy of design. The hermit was a footman – a tradition continued into this century – who would don hair shirt and retreat to the root house as required, to complete the scene.

Stoke Park – 'Among the finest things in England'
Wright designed a garden and park for Charles Bragge at Cleve Hill in Mangots-field, vestiges of which remain, squeezed by suburban development. An octagonal lodge sits incongruously beside the main road; fragments of plantations and even remnants of drives survive. Recently a Kent seat has been identified, standing in a back garden, preserved by repeated coats of thick gloss paint, and still identifiably sited as on Wright's plan. However, Wright's major work in Avon, perhaps in the country, was at Stoke Park outside Bristol (Fig. 27).

Fig. 27. Stoke Park, a pre-1760 watercolour formerly attributed to Paul Sandby.

Wright worked here over a thirty-year period, first for Norborne Berkeley, from 1750 until 1768, when Berkeley left to become Governor of Virginia – by which time the landscape was essentially complete – and then for Berkeley's sister, the 4th Duchess of Beaufort, until his death in 1786.

Berkeley had inherited an agricultural estate of fields and coppice woods, supported by revenue from the Kingswood collieries. He began with tree-planting on the Purdown slopes, and removing the hedges of the fields, but then called in Wright in 1749. The two men developed a close friendship, going on tour together in the north of England to inspect the latest gardens, and writing delighted letters back to Berkeley's sister. Wright introduced a Gothick eyecatcher on Barn Hill, a classical Temple of Horatii and Curiatii on the ridge facing the house across the park, a root house in Hermitage Wood, a ruined castle on the edge of Stapleton village (the tower now part of the former Purdown hospital) and, most characteristically, a series of woodland gardens within the plantations, which became Stoke's most famous feature. Paths up and down steps and through tunnels connected 'saloons' and 'cabinets' decorated with flower beds, statuary, seats and urns. Earth-moving and planting emphasised the sensuous rise and fall of the hills.

At the same time Wright was remodelling the house, a process which eventually saw the whole of the sixteenth-century building encased within the present structure; with its octagon towers and crenellations rising out of embosoming plantations, it would have looked like a fairy castle. In 1756, an Ionic rotunda went up in Barn Wood, and soon after, a memorial in the form of a classical sarcophagus to his brother-in-law. The sarcophagus was restored by the Avon Gardens Trust in 1988. In 1761, an obelisk was built on Star Hill to provide another eyecatcher from the house, while a bridge was thrown across Stoke Lane to connect

STOKE, NEAR BRISTOL.

Fig. 28. Stoke Park from Barn Wood, an aquatint of 1802, showing the house as altered by Wright.

the gardens to a great viewing terrace round Sims Hill, restored in 1993 by Avon County Council and the Countryside Commission.

By 1764 the house was finished, and Wright may have withdrawn from detailed involvement. Certainly the focal point of the landscape, the lake, was the last addition, and there is no evidence to connect it with Wright. Filled in during the construction of the motorway, this is now being restored by the Duchess Lake Fishing Syndicate and the Stoke Park Restoration Trust.

Stoke Park, 'reckon'd among the finest things in England', as Bishop Pococke noted in 1764, was much admired by visitors such as the Duchess of Northumberland and John Wesley; the view from the house was, and still is, breathtaking: such a 'more than semi-circle of Prospect', thought Lady Anson in 1755, surpassing 'the richest as well as the greatest Views I ever saw'.

Lady Nature's Second Husband

The landscape garden, the notion of a whole landscape being a garden, really came into its own in the middle of the eighteenth century, fostered by the indefatigable Lancelot 'Capability' Brown (1716–83), who called his art 'place-making'. Brown invariably took advantage of pre-existing features such as ancient trees, but his work also involved dramatic changes: making lakes in depressions, demolishing terraces in favour of grassy slopes, and famously – and not always conveniently – bringing the park up to the very door. Above all, he planted up parkland in new configurations, with precisely located clumps and groups of trees which emphasised natural contours and seductively drew the eye into the landscape composition. The result was an image of apparently artless beauty, and the common twentieth-century misunderstanding of Brown's work was anticipated by Horace Walpole in his eulogy on Brown's death: 'so closely did he copy nature, that his works will be mistaken'. Walpole mourned him as 'Lady Nature's second husband'.

Kingsweston – the gardens removed, and 'Mr Southil's fine woods'

While some owners initially resisted the new style, as the century went on it became a steamroller. At Kingsweston, change when it came was rapid. In 1764, Bishop Pococke remarked as he passed by on his travels that Mr Southwell was making a park around his house, 'by removing the Stable offices and gardens which are very extensive'. An estate map of 1772 shows how comprehensive the changes were: Vanbrugh's house stands in an informal park of 309 acres/123 hectares, with a perimeter belt of trees. Avenues, gardens, walls, terraces really had been swept away.

Edward Southwell II had begun altering the layout – with some advice from Norborne Berkeley and Thomas Wright who rode over from Stoke Park – in the early 1750s, but after he died in 1755 his son commissioned advice from Brown. Brown's work was for 'Alterations about the House and Terras', which suggests that it was a modest commission. But in the 1760s Southwell was proceeding apace with more extensive landscaping, and Thomas Wright was back at Kingsweston

Fig. 29. Kingsweston – a lithograph of c.1825 showing the view back towards the house from Penpole Lodge.

in 1776. A year later, Southwell died. He was succeeded by his son who was only ten at the time, so the work is likely to have halted then.

The eighteenth-century landscape is depicted in two beautiful watercolours by Nicholas Pocock, and it became one of the great sights on the western tour. The inn, which still survives, connected to the park by the iron bridge over the road, was in itself an attraction – a favourite destination for parties from the Hot Wells – for its hospitality and fine views. Arthur Young advised that for the best prospect you had to go up the hill a little way behind it, from which point 'you look down . . . upon some fine woods, in the midst of which, Mr Southil's house appears' (Plate 11).

Prior Park – from Pope to Brown

The changes at Prior Park under Brown's influence, if not direction, illustrate the change in thinking about gardens in the mid eighteenth century. In the 1750s Allen made a number of improvements to his Popean garden. These included the construction of a cascade below the circular pool, and knocking down walls to extend the landscape down to the old fishponds, over which he had a copy of the Wilton Palladian bridge built (Plate 38). But he then sought the advice of Capability Brown. The extent of Brown's involvement is uncertain, but by the time Allen died in 1764 a classic Brownian landscape had been made, with smooth slopes and curvaceous woods emphasising the vertiginous prospect down to the elegant bridge

Fig. 30. Sham Castle, in a postcard of c.1910.

and lake and away over Bath.

Sham Castle (Fig. 30) was erected as an eyecatcher in 1762, probably by Brown to a design of the amateur architect and pioneer of the Gothick, Sanderson Miller. Miller also worked at Siston Court. He was related by marriage to the Trotman family who owned Siston Court, and the squat ogee-domed lodges have been attributed to him. An engraving of *c.*1805 shows a romantic pleasure ground with a Gothick summerhouse which may also have been Miller's (Fig. 31).

Kelston Park – Wood, Brown and the king's surgeon
Brown's simplest layout in Avon is at Kelston, where Caesar Hawkins, George III's surgeon, had commissioned a new house by John Wood the Younger on the bluff overlooking the Avon. Brown visited in 1767 and was paid the considerable sum of £500 for his work there. For such a price he may have acted as contractor for the work itself, for Brown had his own team of labourers. The 1822 Greenwood map of Somerset shows that the parkland boundary excluded the site of the old manor house, and that here the old avenues were retained. Brown also appears to have retained the northern end of the avenue that ran from the old manor to Summerhouse Wood, as part of an approach to the new house from Kelston village. The park can be clearly viewed from the Bath to Bristol road.

Newton Park – 'finished with great attention'
At Newton Park across the valley, Brown was employed to create a suitable setting for the new house built in 1760 for Joseph Gore Langton, probably by Stiff Leadbetter. Remains of the old castellated house, the keep and gatehouse, were

Fig. 31. An engraving of Fiennes Trotman's drawing of c.1805 (from Fosbroke's Gloucestershire, 1807), showing the new Gothick setting of Siston Court.

retained as was the fashion, not only as a picturesque feature but as a symbol of the family's pedigree. Newton Park contains an interesting example of a Brownian walk around a pleasure ground, into which he introduced a chain of three lakes, created by a dam across the Corston Brook – the lowest is now silted up. The pleasure ground would have been mown rather than grazed like parkland, and would thus have been able to accommodate specimen trees and shrubs.

The park he remodelled in typical style, although he retained fragments of the earlier avenues at a distance from the house. Repton commented that Newton Park was a spot which Brown was 'supposed to have finished with great attention'. Although Repton then went on to suggest improvements, the landscape's greatest debt is to Brown. Today, it still retains the spacious calm of a Brownian composition; a public footpath runs through the park.

Dodington – and the Beautiful
Brown was also engaged at Dodington, and in 1764 and 1767 he had two contracts worth £1,368. From the River Frome he made two lakes with a weir between them; he planted hanging beech woods on the hillsides, opened up valleys, and wound a driveway through the trees and lawns. Brown made a serpentine aqueduct to a castellated cascade into the lake, and James Wyatt introduced a garden pavilion as a waterside feature. With its sensuous curves and swellings, Dodington perfectly fulfils Edmund Burke's definition of the Beautiful: the sense 'of being swiftly drawn

in an easy coach, on a smooth turf, with gradual ascents and declivities' (Plate 12). The landscape also bears an uncanny resemblance to the Brown landscape as caricatured later in the century by the high priest of the Picturesque, Richard Payne Knight. Dodington is unfortunately not open to the public, but footpaths do skirt the parkland.

Amateurs, Eccentrics and Quakers

It is simple but misleading to see history in terms of a few big names and sites. Of course the majority of parks and gardens were not laid out by Kent or Brown. They were created by the owners and their own staff on an *ad hoc* basis. While this often meant a pale imitation of the Brownian or Kentian style, a number of amateurs were directed by vivid ideas of their own and the stimulus of their own circle of friends. Undistracted by the dictates of professional consultants, they created unique gardens and parks as a result.

Ham Green – 'Mr Bright's Pleasure ground'
One such garden was Ham Green on the banks of the Avon. Richard Bright had bought the Queen Anne house here in the 1730s or 1740s, and by 1789, when it was depicted by the itinerant artist Samuel Hieronymus Grimm, 'Mr Bright's Pleasure ground' was a miniature Arcadia. Dates are uncertain, but the hexagonal Gothick gazebo with its ogee windows and battlements and fine view up-river to the wooded gorge has been attributed to the American-born architect James Bridges, which would date it *c.*1760 (Plate 13). It seems to have been Bright's son, also Richard (born 1754), who had the horticultural interests, but this tentative dating would make the gazebo the elder Bright's creation. In 1789, Bright junior converted the gazebo into a laboratory, in which he did much of the research on the disease which now bears his name.

Apart from the gazebo, the riverside folly known as Adam and Eve was built by the time of Grimm's visit. A ha-ha was constructed and a wide variety of ornamental trees planted. The garden and hothouse at Ham Green were full of rarities – Bright made a gift of pineapples to the Polish revolutionary Kosciuszko as he passed down the Avon on his way to America in 1797. The serpentine lake in the valley below the garden may have been Bright's creation too.

Midford Castle – 'highly picturesque and romantic'
Another highly individual garden was laid out by Henry Disney Roebuck in about 1775, around his Gothick castle on the bluff above Midford. In plan the castle might well be modelled on Blaise, but its elevation is more playful and more mock-castle than Blaise. Collinson described it thus in 1791:

> On the north and east sides of the house is a very deep narrow sequestered glen, the steep sides of which are clothed with fine coppice woods intersected with beautiful walks ornamented with flowering shrubs. On an abrupt part of the brow, which overlooks the hollow, at the bottom of which a brook

murmurs along a rocky channel, the proprietor has erected an elegant building called the Priory, with Gothick windows and a circular embattled tower, in which is a commodious tea-room and offices below. At a little distance from this, under a thick mass of shade stands a rustic hermitage on the brow of the steep descent. The whole surrounding scenery is highly picturesque and romantic.

After 1810, further buildings were added for the new owner, including a Gothick greenhouse, gate piers and lodge. These survive, as does the Strawberry Hill Gothick Priory, and many of the ornamental walks, although without their flowering shrubs; the rustic hermitage has disappeared without a trace. Since 1901 the estate has been in divided ownership; Priory Woods is now owned by the Fuller's Earth Co.

The society of merchant-gardeners

Four Gothick gardens were laid out near Bristol in the mid eighteenth century by owners with shared religious or business connections. The Society of Friends in Bristol was a small community which played a disproportionately dynamic role in the city's industrial development. Three of the Friends, Thomas Goldney III, William Champion and William Reeve, also devoted much time, money and imagination to their gardens, stocking them with bizarre architectural curiosities. Reeve was also on close terms with the Society of Merchant Venturers, of which a leading light was Thomas Farr; in 1762, Farr bought the estate at Henbury which was to become Blaise Castle. There is no doubt that they were all known to each other, and one can imagine how ideas would have swirled about this group.

The Quaker and trade connections of Bristol with North America also meant the area was well placed to take advantage of the latest imported exotics. In the mid eighteenth century the key figure in the import of American plants was the Quaker Peter Collinson, who was supplied by the tireless plant collector John Bartram of Pennsylvania. The first appearance in England of such American plants as *Rhododendron maximum*, *Magnolia acuminata*, bergamot, many species of aster, phlox and solidago, red, black and white oaks, sugar and silver maples, may well have been on the quays of Bristol.

Goldney – 'a stupendous work'

Thomas Goldney had inherited his father's banking and money-lending business, and made a great deal of money investing in trade, including privateering and even guns after the Spanish war was declared. He had inherited the estate in 1731, and in 1736 he began to keep a garden book recording planting and works. A garden with 'Walks, Greens, Water-works, Summer-Houses &c.' already existed, and it may well be that Goldney kept this earlier framework intact, even while adding more land and introducing a host of new features.

The grotto was the most extraordinary feature of the garden, and it was twenty-seven years in the making – an almost obsessive work. Started as a simple underground passage under a public footpath, connecting the garden to the first additional parcel of land that Goldney bought, endless elaborations resulted in the phenomenon that survives today (Plate 14). Virtually every visitor who recorded his or her impressions expressed astonishment – although not always unqualified admiration. Arthur Young found it 'curious in materials and taste', and thought the terror associated with the lion out of place in a 'sequestered grot'. The variety and rarity of many of the fossils, shells and minerals used by Goldney were, however, 'better of their sort, than in any grotto I have seen'. John Wesley pronounced that it was 'the largest and most beautiful in its kind that I ever saw'.

Goldney, unmarried and temperamental, seems to have been reluctant to show the grotto and his gardens. Young refers to his 'affectation of keeping them locked

Fig. 32. Goldney on its eminence, as shown in a view from Granby Hill by Lt. Col. William Booth, 1822.

up from common eyes'; and Mrs Delany, another notable garden tourist, reported that he was famous as a niggard, although 'she was so fortunate as to take his fancy' and was let in. After Goldney's death in 1768 his sister allowed entry to the grotto by ticket, and by the end of the century it had become a famous tourist attraction, warranting a whole page of description in Shiercliff's *Bristol and Hotwell Guide* of 1793.

The garden made the most of its spectacular situation, and the view from the prospect was much praised. The Duchess of Northumberland thought it a 'stupendous work'. The view was further enhanced by Goldney's construction of the gazebo and the Gothick prospect tower of 1764, which doubled up as his 'fire engine', housing a steam-powered pump that raised water for the cascade in the grotto and for the fountain which formerly played in the canal. Below the gazebo he had mock fortifications built, with a walk on top. The terrace and bastion allowed him to command – the word seems apt – the whole of the harbour below, into which his ships brought their valuable cargoes (Fig. 32).

The garden, the core of which has not changed substantially since the eighteenth century, is geometrical in design, with the canal and yew avenue at right angles to the great viewing terrace. Shiercliff's guide remarked that the garden was 'in the old taste', but it was remarkably popular, and the guide advertised tickets.

Warmley and William Champion – 'no queerer mortal'
William Champion was a dynamic entrepreneur. After travelling abroad to study various metallurgical processes, he moved to Warmley in 1746, to pioneer the new industrial techniques. Evidently he was a difficult man to get on with; a business associate said that he knew 'no queerer mortal'. But in twenty years he built up at Warmley the world's largest industrial estate: 79 acres/32 hectares of furnaces, mills, presses, assembly shops and workers' cottages. By 1769 he was bankrupt and forced to sell the entire concern, but while at Warmley he found time to build himself a house and to create a garden similar in many ways to Goldney's.

North-west of his house, a 13-acre/11-hectare lake was made by damming Siston Brook; a smaller semi-circular pond provided a formal element within the garden. Close to the pond, Champion built an extensive system of underground chambers and tunnels, vaulted and arched and enlivened with cascades. Archaeological investigations by Lesley Howes for the Kingswood Museum Trust suggest that Champion was utilising redundant industrial features in making the grotto. The walls were lined with iridescent black clinker, a by-product of his copper smelting. It is not certain whether this was the intended final appearance of the grotto, or whether further elaboration was cut short by Champion's bankruptcy. Champion bought his first steam-engine in 1749 (well before Goldney bought his) and used it to circulate water from his mills back to the lake and through the grotto. He made a spectacle of this process, as witnessed by *Felix Farley's Bristol Journal*:

> The machine is the most noblest of its kind in the world; it discharges upwards of 3,000 hogsheads of water in an hour; the water is buoyed up by several tubes in a Hemispherical Form, and falls into the pool as a cascade; and affords a grand and beautiful scene.

Black slag formed into blocks was also used to build a small castellated Gothick summerhouse over the Siston Brook. This may well have proved the inspiration for the Black Castle, built later at Arno's Court, which used just such blocks. A straight Elm Walk led along the lake towards the summerhouse, while a mount was located at the southern end of the lake, overlooking the whole complex of pleasure grounds and industrial site.

The presiding genius of Champion's garden was the god Neptune, who stood on an island in the middle of the lake. The statue's chief distinction was its enormous size. Although the lake has been drained, Neptune survives, minus his trident, and he is perhaps more striking now amid the caravans than he was on his island. But this must have been quite a sight in Champion's time – the elegant classical box of a house, the grotto, the thundering cascade, Neptune and the enormous lake, with the blazing furnaces and belching chimneys behind. The house is now a nursing home, but Kingswood Borough Council and the local volunteers have done much to repair and interpret the gardens which are now a public open space.

Blaise Castle – 'far superior to Stowe'

Blaise Castle at Henbury (Plate 37) is now chiefly associated with Humphry Repton, but in the 1760s and 1770s the American merchant Thomas Farr created a great landscape garden there, compared by visitors to the finest in the country – 'far superior to Stowe gardens', commented John Wesley.

In 1762 Farr bought the old gabled manor house and part of the fragmented estate of the Great House, including Blaise Hill and the gorge of the Hazel Brook (Fig. 33). Until he was bankrupted by the American war and forced to sell in 1778, he devoted much of his energy to creating a spectacular landscape. His model was Piercefield, the 'Sublime' layout on the Wye above Chepstow, with its dizzying

Fig. 33. The gorge at Blaise, drawn by S.H. Grimm in 1788, showing the castle and the bastion, now demolished.

cliff-top walks and evocatively named features: Lover's Leap, the Giant's Cave, Druid's Temple. At Henbury, Farr saw the capabilities of the gorge, and laid out walks which took full advantage of its dramatic potential. He also attempted to force the brook into more than its placid flow, with various weirs and culvertings – to little effect, according to Repton.

The Castle (Fig. 34 and Plate 37) was built in 1766, and the building draws on two fashions – the watchtower or belvedere, and the sham castle, sometimes built in an evocatively ruinous state. Sanderson Miller was designing ruins in 1747 at Hagley in Worcestershire, and nearer home had designed Sham Castle for Ralph Allen at Prior Park in 1762. At Badminton, Thomas Wright's Ragged Castle had been built by about 1750, and nearer Bristol his ruin at Stoke Park was probably built within the next ten years. In about 1763 or 1764, William Reeve was building the Black Castle at Arno's Court, but Goldney's Gothick tower of 1764 seems the most obvious model.

At Blaise, the Castle was the centrepiece of the pleasure garden, whether in its role as a picturesque object 'embosom'd high in tufted trees', or as the culmination of the wood walks. It was designed for more than just looking out from: the inventory of 1789 lists its rooms as cellar, bedroom, kitchen, lobby, china pantry and drawing room, and it was inhabited by an estate worker until the 1920s.

Fig. 34. Watercolour of Blaise Castle in 1827 by J.M. Field.

Other buildings in the grounds were in a mixture of styles: a rustic root house in the manner of Thomas Wright; a classical alcove and bath house by the brook (its foundations are now the 'Giant's Soapdish'). Below the castle, overlooking the gorge, he had built a series of battlements, which seem to have been called 'bastions', no doubt again in imitation of Goldney's bastion.

The drama was heightened still further by Farr's use of local (and no doubt invented) legends – Lover's Leap, Giant Goram's Chair, the Robbers' Cave, Echo Gate. This was a landscape of 'delicious terror', and it is fitting to think that the philosopher who defined 'the Sublime', Edmund Burke, must have walked with his friend Thomas Farr along the Blaise walks when he stayed here during his election campaign in 1774.

Arno's Court and the devil's cathedral

William Reeve, Quaker businessman and industrialist, lived at Arno's Court on the rising ground above the foundries and furnaces in Crew's Hole beside the Avon, from which much of his wealth seems to have derived. Here he built a Gothick villa and an extravagant collection of ornamental buildings, partly in parkland, partly in a pleasure garden cut off from the house by the Bath road.

The Black Castle certainly housed stables, laundry and various offices, but its size makes it a cuckoo of a garden building – Walpole called it the 'Devil's Cathedral' (Plate 41). It was approached from the house via a Gothick archway, ornamented with medieval statues that Reeve had salvaged from the demolition of

Fig. 35. The Gothick bath house at Arno's Court, painted by T.L.S. Rowbotham, 1826/7.

Lawford's Gate and Newgate in Bristol. Reeve also had an extraordinary rococo Gothick bath house built, reached via a subterranean grotto tunnel under the road; he may also have been responsible for the formal terraced garden and bath house at Crew's Hole off Strawberry Lane – the latter presumably superseded by the more elaborate construction nearer the house. In the parkland behind the house, a summerhouse overlooked the whole composition.

The bath house (Fig. 35) with its chinoiserie plasterwork of dolphins, water gods and sea shells has gone, removed to Portmeirion by Clough Williams-Ellis before it disintegrated entirely. Today, the archway and the Black Castle would benefit from a similar rescue operation, as the development corporation's spine road obliterates the last semblance of Reeve's layout, and the castle finds itself marooned between dual carriageway and shopping centre car park.

The Communal and Public Gardens of Bristol and Bath

The town gardens of Bristol and Bath can be divided into those that are private and those that were planned as public or communal open spaces. In both cities, urban expansion in the eighteenth century was designed around the public spaces.

The largest of these sites is Queen Square in Bristol, named to commemorate the visit of Queen Anne in 1702. The centrepiece of the redevelopment of the Marsh area, it was made into a formal garden in 1716, with diagonal gravel paths and three rows of lime trees around the edge – two hundred and forty were planted in that year. With the installation of Rysbrack's fine statue of William III in 1736, the square was complete (Plate 15).

Unlike Bath, Bristol's Georgian town planning has been largely destroyed in the twentieth century; and of course Bristol never lent itself to master planning of the sort carried out by John Wood, or proposed by others, such as Thomas Baldwin's plans for the Bathwick estate. It was more piecemeal in Bristol and only fragments remain. But it is still possible to stroll from Portland Square (begun in 1790) with its fine mature lime, horse chestnut and plane trees, into Brunswick Square (1788) and thence along Cumberland Street, which once led to St James's Square (begun 1708), before finding yourself in the cavernous car parks of Avon House North. Dowry Square was built *c*.1721–50 around a communal garden, with the south side left open to the views of the river (now obscured by the main road and the Cumberland Basin flyover). King Square, built between 1740 and 1760, was also laid out around a communal garden; its original cross rows of limes were removed in 1838. Only a fragment of the communal garden of the 1756 Somerset Square in Redcliffe remains, surrounded not by Georgian terraces but by high-rise flats. However, the eccentric central fountain dates from the mid to late eighteenth century, and has even been ascribed to Thomas Wright.

John Wood and the gardens of Bath
John Wood described at length the garden laid out in Queen Square in Bath after 1728:

The ground of the square is inclosed with a low wall bearing a Balustrade; and in the middle of every side there are gates of twenty feet broad, with Peers on each side of them. Next to the Balustrade there is a border of flowers; a Bason, of forty five feet diameter, makes the centre of the whole area . . . The four quarters of the square are planted with flowering shrubs. The walks next the Balustrade, and from Gate to Gate, are laid with gravel; a verge of grass next the hedges separates the diagonal from the other walks; and those diagonal walks are covered with turf, whose Verdure is always pleasing to the Eye, and very much adds to the Beauty of the Square.

The inclosing, planting, turfing and gravelling this open area, in the manner above described, was a work of much greater expence than the paving the whole surface of it would have been and the trees planted in it eclipse a great part of the Basement of the Building on one side, from such as view it on the opposite side. But yet I preferred an inclosed square to an open one, to make this as useful as possible: For the intention of a Square in a City is for people to assemble together; and the spot whereon they meet, ought to be separated from the ground common to Men and Beasts, and even to mankind in general, if decency and good order are necessary to be observed in such places of Assembly; of which, I think, there can be no doubt.

Wood clearly felt ambivalent about the presence of the garden in the square. It interfered with the architecture, and it also compromised his Roman ideal of the square's function as a place of public assembly. Instead, Queen Square was dominated by a very private and secluded garden, divided from the masses by a formidable balustrade crowned with obelisks.

Wood's next major development, from 1738, was the Parades. North and South Parade were the first in England to be so called, highlighting the indivisibility of the terraced housing and the walks, built as they were in suitable proximity to the fashionable parades of Harrison's Walks and the Grove. North Parade was intended for use during the summer, when it was shaded by the houses on its southern side, with stairs leading down into a garden in James's Triangle, now Parade Gardens. Wood designed an unexecuted plan for the garden, based on a circle with three equidistant entrances, with a Summer Garden in the centre and a broad Spring Walk below the retaining wall of the Parade.

South Parade was intended for autumn and winter use, catching whatever sunshine there was. It was also expected to overlook the Royal Forum, but this never developed beyond a few utilitarian gardens. The view from both Parades is now urban in character, but in the eighteenth century the pastoral beauty of the river landscape was recorded by artists and writers alike. Fanny Burney, lodging in one of the houses in 1780, wrote: 'We have meadows, hills, Prior Park, the soft-flowing Avon – whatever nature has to offer, I think, always in our view' (Plate 16). From the end of South Parade a ferry crossed the river to walks in the meadows.

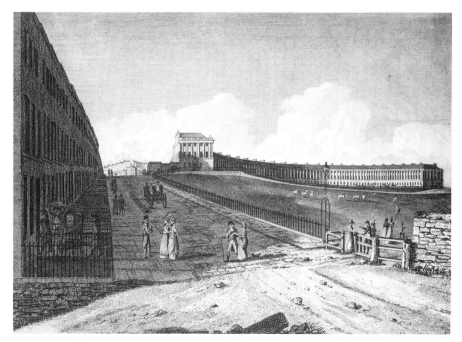

Fig. 36. Royal Crescent – a mansion rising out of a lawn like a composition by Capability Brown. An engraving of 1801 by Jacob Spornberg.

The greatest union of landscape and building in Bath is surely the Royal Crescent, built to Wood the Younger's design between 1767 and 1774. Fanny Burney again wrote of how the Crescent, 'to all the excellence of architecture that adorns the Circus adds all the delights of nature that beautify the Parade'. Christopher Pound has observed how the Crescent rises out of the ground like a great mansion rising from a Brown park. It seems possible that Wood and Brown were working together at Kelston Park nearby at about the time work began on the Crescent, and a Brownian influence can be seen in the smooth lawn which from the south appears to stretch right up to the building itself (Fig. 36).

Private town gardens – 'bounded places'

In his influential *Ichnographia Rustica* (1718 and 1742), the garden theorist Stephen Switzer made a clear distinction between the planting and design suitable for a country estate, and that suitable for a town garden, making clear where his priorities lay. He thought 'Clipt Plants, Flowers, and other trifling Decorations fit only for little Town gardens, and not for the expansive Tracts of the Country', but did not 'condemn all Enclosed and Flower Gardens, since they are absolutely necessary in Cities, Towns and other bounded places'.

In the great architectural set pieces of squares and crescents of the first half of the century, little attention was paid to the private gardens. While Queen Square in Bristol is over 7 acres/3 hectares in extent, the back 'garden' of a Colonel Yate's house in the adjoining Prince Street was only 35 x 45 feet/10.5 x 13.5 metres. And it would probably have merely been paved, as advised by Isaac Ware in his *Complete Body of Architecture* (1756):

> Some attempt to make flower gardens of these little plots, but this is very idle: plants require a purer air than animals, and however we breathe in London, they cannot live where there is so much smoke and confinement: nor will even gravel continue many days from the turning. In this respect therefore, instead of borders under the walls, the best method is to lay the whole with good sound stone pavement.

However, the Bath Archaeological Trust's remarkable excavation in 1985 of the garden to the rear of 4 The Circus (built in 1758) revealed stone-flagged walks, beds, gravel instead of a lawn, and the footings of a trellis screen. All this has now been restored.

Occasionally, the façades of the buildings located at the end of these terraced gardens were given an ornamental treatment, as in the temple façade to the stable building behind 13 Royal Crescent in Bath, designed by Wood the Younger, or the Palladian façade behind 7 King Square in Bristol – visible from the street because the garden has been turned into a car park.

Occasionally, too, more elaborate structures were fitted into the gardens behind these houses. Thomas Robins recorded the Gothick folly in the garden of Dr Oliver's house in Queen Square, Bath, only in part functioning as a screen to the stables. In the garden of 21 Queen Square there was a free-standing summerhouse, until it was incorporated into extensions to the house.

By the latter half of the eighteenth century, houses in the fashionable parts of Bath were being provided with fairly generous gardens, as recorded on the Harcourt Masters map of 1794–5. By this date, the principles of landscape and picturesque gardening were infiltrating into town gardens, and Harcourt Masters illustrates a wide, even anarchic, range of designs to the rear of the uniform terraces and squares. Oval and circular beds or lawns, asymmetrical serpentine paths and shrubberies all feature within the rectangular plots. However, the majority remained rectilinear, fulfilling the observation made by Loudon in his *Suburban Gardener* of 1838:

> It must be obvious, that, in gardens of so regular a shape, whether large or small, there can be very little variety produced in laying them out; that the style adopted must be regular . . . and chief interest must depend on the trees and plants introduced.

Although a date of 1840 is assigned to it, the painting of the garden of the old Red Maids' School in Denmark Street in Bristol nevertheless gives us an excellent idea of the appearance of a town garden at the end of the eighteenth century (Plate 17). As a school mistress's garden it might be expected to be old-fashioned, and indeed its layout accords with the design of 4 The Circus, and the gardens were of similar proportions. Like the Circus garden, the Red Maids' consists of a number of flower beds arranged in a simple geometrical pattern in an expanse of gravel, with borders under the walls. The beds and borders are edged with dwarf box, and in the central beds are some small shrubs of regular clipped outline. There is a rather spindly lilac tree and some roses in the right-hand border. The other planting is not so easily identifiable, but there appear to be flowers, perhaps annuals, in the central beds, climbers on the house, and plants in pots on the first-floor windowsill.

Loudon's observation on the importance of the flowers themselves in town gardens is borne out by evidence of the continuing interest in the development of florists' flowers described in the previous chapter. An advertisement in the *Bath Chronicle* in June 1779 for a house to let in Lansdown Road includes a description of the garden, and concludes:

Whereas the said Garden has been robbed of a the prime flower-roots, such as, ranunculuses, hyacinths, anemonies, &c., and the Canal of its gold and silver fish, tench, carp, &c., – Whoever will discover the person or persons who committed the said robbery, so that he, she, or they may be brought to justice, shall upon conviction recieve Ten Guineas reward . . .

Collectors' flowers commanded high prices at that time. A catalogue of 1777 lists prices for auriculas from 1s to £2.2s, and hyacinths from 2s to a staggering £21 for 'Black Flora'. All across the country there were keenly attended shows and competitions, usually held with an annual florists' feast. The *Gloucester Journal* records florists' feasts in Bath as early as 1742 and 1743, at which the prize for the winning carnations was a set of silver knee and shoe buckles. The *Bath Chronicle* in 1780 carries advertisements for 'The Annual AURICULA FLORISTS FEAST', and a similar advert for the annual carnation feast. Bristol too had its florists: the *Bristol Journal* for 1772, for example, records two auricula feasts, one of the winners being 'Severn's Fame', shown by Mr Sixsmith, gardener to Gabriel Goldney Esq.

Gardens on the edge of town

For city dwellers, an alternative to communal gardens was an entirely separate garden on the edge of town; such gardens were common around large towns and cities in the second half of the eighteenth century. One writer, describing the outskirts of Birmingham in 1803, recorded, 'in every direction . . . a zone of vegetable beauty in which are stuck by way of grotesque ornaments, arbours and summer-houses of all the forms that untutored fancy can devise'; there were 'upwards of a thousand gardens' forming 'a Chinese view, with little fanciful temples and various arbourage, calculated for recreation and use'. Although in size they were comparable to allotments (being generally between 1/6 and 1/8 of an acre/1,600 to 1,250 square metres), they were laid out primarily as pleasure gardens, with elaborate paths and beds, and ornamental buildings. These buildings could even function as holiday and weekend homes. Loudon wrote in 1831 of the planting of one such garden, that the immense selection of hardy shrubs and plants 'quite astonished us'.

Rocque's 1742 map of Bristol shows many such gardens around the edge of the city, complete with fancy layouts and summerhouses (Fig. 37). An advertisement

Plate 11. Kingsweston, c.1785, by Nicholas Pocock – a view from the point advised by Arthur Young showing the house in its landscape setting and its dramatic prospects.

Plate 12. Dodington: smooth, shaven and serpentine – fulfilling the notion of beauty promoted by Burke and by Brown.

Plate 13. Ham Green gazebo, restored by the Avon Gardens Trust in 1988.

Plate 14. The grotto at Goldney – John Wesley admired its exceptional beauty.

Plate 15. Queen Square, Bristol painted by T.L.S. Rowbotham in 1827 showing newly-planted lime trees among mature trees of the 1716 planting.

Plate 16. The view from North Parade in Bath over the Avon and its meadows as depicted by Elizabeth Clayborn Crossley in a print of 1759.

Plate 17. The Red Maids' School, Denmark St, Bristol. Anonymous painting, c.1840.

Plate 18. Timber Lodge on the drive at Blaise – although of uncertain date, the influence of Thomas Wright is unmistakeable.

Plate 19. Blaise Hamlet, as depicted by Francis Danby soon after it was built.

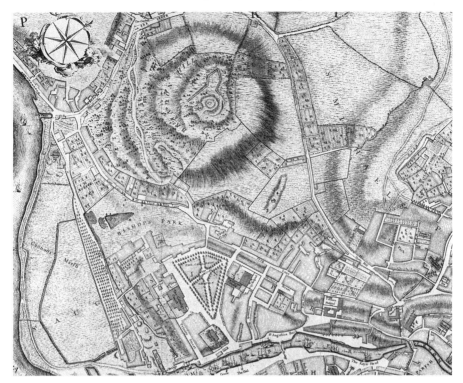

Fig. 37. A detail of Rocque's map of Bristol, 1742, showing detached gardens on the edge of the city.

in Bonner and Middleton's *Bristol Journal* in April 1786 gives us a little more information about these gardens:

> A GARDEN / To be LETT immediately / a Neat little GARDEN, near this City, well walled in, with Wall and other Fruit Trees, and a beautiful little Summer-House newly built, situated at a Place called the Tennis-Court, in the Parish of St Philip and Jacob.

A plan of a garden on the edge of Bath, dating from the early nineteenth century and occupied by a Captain Hue, corresponds with this description remarkably closely. Of the plants tantalisingly identified by initials only, the 'a's are presumably apples, and the numerous 'c's and 'g's perhaps currants and gooseberries, but the layout is clearly intended to be ornamental as well as functional. These gardens were much prized, and when leases were sold, they could exchange hands for as much as sixty guineas – no doubt the plan described was drawn up at the time of such a sale.

Chapter 4

The Picturesque and the Early Nineteenth Century, 1783–1837

PICTURESQUE TRAVEL, the cult of seeing English countryside in terms of framed views and visual compositions, was inspired by the publication in 1782 of the Reverend William Gilpin's tour of the Wye. The concept of the Picturesque as an aesthetic category soon developed, to complement the Sublime and the Beautiful, and it meant rough, rugged or irregular. Artists whose work set the standard were Salvator Rosa, the Dutch realists, and Claude Lorrain. The Picturesque eschewed conventional images of beauty in favour of objects such as a rustic bridge, a gnarled old tree, a jagged cliff, an ivy-clad ruin, a shaggy peasant cottage (or even a shaggy peasant).

The best disquisition on the Picturesque takes place on Beechen Cliff overlooking Bath, when Jane Austen's Henry Tilney lectures Catherine Morland in *Northanger Abbey*: 'He talked of foregrounds, distances, and second distances – side-screens and perspectives – lights and shades – and Catherine was so hopeful a scholar, that when they gained the top of Beechen Cliff, she voluntarily rejected the whole city of Bath, as unworthy to make part of the landscape.'

It was not long before the theorists sought to apply picturesque principles to landscape gardening, promoting ruggedness and roughness in planting and buildings. Brown's smoothness soon became the butt of much criticism, and the great designer of this period, Humphry Repton, was tarred with the same brush. But in fact Repton, as he moved away from Brown, fulfilled many of the ideals of the picturesque camp: in retaining and capitalising on features such as old trees – even avenues – or buildings, in introducing incidents and human activity into the compositions, and in developing viewpoints or 'stations', as Gilpin termed them. Indeed, his whole approach in his famous Red Books, in which he presented his

Fig. 38. A picturesque little building in a picturesque setting: the hermitage at Wick House, Brislington, by T.L.S. Rowbotham, 1826/7.

alterations as a series of pictures, was picturesque. Blaise and Oldbury Court exemplify his picturesque style perfectly.

Humphry Repton – Nature reconquered

Capability Brown died in 1783, and Repton, very consciously his successor, took up the mantle in 1788. Brown's imitators continued working in his style after his death, but Repton, although so conscious of Brown's shadow, was gradually developing his own ideas on the laying out of both parks and gardens; especially after teaming up with the ambitious architect John Nash, he was defining a new landscape aesthetic. By the time of his death in 1818, Repton had modified the Brownian formula into something with more incident, ornament and variety, with more elaborate forms of water and plantations. Lady Nature's third husband was a great deal less tolerant of her vagaries. As Repton said in his Red Book for Blaise: 'Nature must be conquered by Art, and it is only the ostentation of her triumph, and not her victory, that ought ever to offend the correct Eye of Taste.'

With Repton leading the way by virtue of his powerful clients and his lavish presentations, the taste for more varied scenery in a park was complemented by an increasing tendency to re-establish the garden as an area distinct from the park, not only physically but in character. By the final phase of his career, Repton was creating gardens like Ashridge in Hertfordshire or Endsleigh in Devon, with elaborate formal terraces, pergolas, fountains, geometrical flower beds, trellis work, arcades and even parterres. His proposal for Leigh Court at Abbot's Leigh in 1814 included elaborate terraced kitchen and flower gardens in the Italianate style.

Most distinctive in Repton's aesthetic was a moral element. The end of the eighteenth century was a volatile period in English history. The French revolution had shaken the complacency of the establishment, and the 'old order' of class was cracking up with the drift of the proletariat into the cities and the growth of the trades union movement. This context helps to explain some of the intensity of the controversy over what even then was a backwater in aesthetic theory. Repton was a paternalist Tory by nature. Deploring ostentatious show and exclusiveness – even though he could, when required, turn it on for a client – he made landscapes that were designed to reflect, or perhaps commemorate, an ideal relationship between landlord and tenant. Thus, where Brown had often sought to screen or even remove dwellings from his views, Repton liked pretty cottages – often they had to be specially built and sited to be pretty enough – as elements in his compositions.

The combes of Bath and the gorges of Bristol, as well as the topography of areas such as the Mendips, make Avon naturally picturesque. There are a number of layouts in the county which are picturesque by virtue of little more than winding paths past natural features such as outcrops of rock, cliffs and river gorges. Repton carried out many commissions around Bath and Bristol – to date his involvement has been identified in ten sites in Avon – and amateurs, too, created some remarkable landscapes at this time.

Repton's ingenious sales technique, his Red Books, give us a unique record of the methods he used. Invited by a landowner to tender for a job, Repton would provide a red morocco-bound book containing a hand-scripted text, illustrated with his own watercolours, to convey his ideas for the landscape. His prose was a mixture of brisk authority, lyricism and appalling flattery, but what must most often have won the day was his arrangement of 'slides', by which a flap on the painted view of the existing landscape could be lifted to show the landscape as improved. They were beautiful productions, which an owner was pleased to show his friends, and Repton's industry was often repaid with further commissions in the same circle.

Blaise Castle – 'the delights of romantic scenery'

Repton's best known work in Avon is Blaise Castle, which he designed for the Quaker John Scandrett Harford, following a visit in 1795 and a Red Book done a year later. Given a fine existing landscape, Repton did not propose radical change, but did introduce some key new elements, as well as advising on the site for the new house. He did away with the whimsicality of Thomas Farr's bastions and his unsuccessful water features; he cleared new views by 'judicious use of the axe'; but, most critically, he put in a new approach from Henbury Hill, even though

Fig. 39. Repton's Lodge at the entrance to his new approach to Blaise Castle.

the house lay only 100 yards/90 metres from the village street in the other direction (Fig. 39).

This approach not only gave a flattering impression of the estate's extent, it also capitalised on the estate's greatest feature – the gorge. Taking 1 1/2 miles/2.2 kilometres to approach the house, it verges on the ridiculous, but with its Gothick lodge, its rocky outcrops and hairpin bends, its final effect is closer to the Sublime. But this was Nature conquered, and Repton was keen to stress that the road was 'perfectly easy and accessible'. It would, he wrote in the Red Book, 'excite admiration and surprize without any mixture of that terror which tho' it partakes of the sublime, is very apt to destroy the delights of romantic scenery'.

Two features on the present drive – Repton's seems to have been slightly modified in the nineteenth century – are the Woodman's Cottage and Timber Lodge. The former was introduced by Repton as a feature in the views from the house. It would introduce 'ideas of animation and movement', and a note of benevolent paternalism – '*la Simplicité soignée*', as he called it. As a bonus, smoke from its chimney would produce exquisite aesthetic effects in the hanging woods and the glen. Timber Lodge is a marvellous *cottage naturel*, covered entirely with roots, bark and thatch (Plate 18). Its date is uncertain, but it is very similar to the Badminton root house and the now demolished lodge of Stapleton Grove, owned by Joseph Harford. Stapleton Grove lodge could well have been designed by Thomas Wright, who was working on the neighbouring Stoke Park, so it is at least possible that Timber Lodge is a copy of a Wright design.

The desired sense of social harmony was further enhanced by Nash's Blaise

Hamlet, built for J.S. Harford between 1810 and 1811 (Plate 19). Nor was it a superficial show of benevolence. Prince Pückler-Muskau noted on his visit in 1828 that the inhabitants were all poor families who had the cottages rent free, and the plans show that the cottages were built to a high standard, every one having its own privy, copper and oven. The only price was being on show. The cottages were set in a profusion of flowers – clematis, rose, honeysuckle and vine: 'the gardens, divided by neat headges, form a pretty garland of flowers and herbs around twhole village', wrote the Prince. The Hamlet provides a heartening contrast to the evictions associated with the Brownian phase of landscaping, which Oliver Goldsmith described in 'The Deserted Village': 'The country blooms – a garden, and a grave'.

Oldbury Court – 'sublime and beautiful'

Repton's work at Oldbury Court on the banks of the River Frome is less well known, but recent research by the Avon Gardens Trust, and a Countryside Commission's Task Force Trees survey, have revealed the extent to which his layout survives. Walks through the woods above the Frome evidently existed in the late eighteenth century, when the area was a well-known beauty spot. Its natural contours had been made more dramatic by small quarries along its cliffs, and when Repton was called in by a new owner, Thomas Graeme, in 1799, he must have been genuinely impressed. He wrote that 'it would be difficult to select a better

Drawn by H.Repton Esq.r   Engraved by John Pelt.o

The BANKS of the FROME, OLDBURY COURT, near BRISTOL.

Fig. 40. The Frome at Oldbury Court, drawn by Repton for Peacock's Polite Repository, *1803.*

Fig. 41. The lodge at the Frenchay entrance to Oldbury Court, demolished in 1949, from a postcard of 1917.

specimen than Oldbury Court . . . with such a variety of sublime and beautiful scenery as seldom occurs in places of much greater extent' (Fig. 40).

The old gabled house stood in a parkland setting on the level ground above the gorge, and Repton's efforts were concentrated on the woods which led down to the river, clothing the sides of the gorge. One notable feature is a beautifully graded terrace walk, which takes the walker imperceptibly up to a point where the land falls away and a panoramic view encompasses the hanging woods, the river far below, and the embosomed roofs of the riverside village of Frenchay.

Repton appears to have proposed a rotunda on an eminence on that far side of the river, but if it was built, it has disappeared along with the thatched lodge by the bridge at Frenchay (Fig. 41), a boathouse on the river, a cottage and a summerhouse. The brook which falls from the upper park to the Frome was ornamented with pools, bridges and cascades, and rustic bridges also crossed the Frome, where no doubt the mills were also featured as picturesque objects.

The scene remains extraordinarily picturesque still: the paths are intact; the line of Repton's approach from the Frenchay lodge can be traced where it diverges from the present drive; and the walks and caves as romantic as ever. Only recent City Council planting of an unsympathetic character, and the erection of intrusive safety fencing by the river and cliff-top has marred its appearance. Oldbury is a less prestigious site than Blaise, but it is equally picturesque and deserves to be much better known and valued. The hanging woods, full of trees dating from Repton's time, are now in urgent need of maintenance and sympathetic replanting.

Brentry Hill – 'a most pleasing and extensive view'
Brentry Hill (1802) is one of only two sites (the other is Sheringham in Norfolk, now owned by the National Trust), where Repton and his son John Adey Repton produced designs for house and landscape together. In his *Observations on the theory and practice of landscape gardening* (1803), Repton wrote that 'few houses have been built with more attention to the situation and circumstances of the place than the villa at Brentry'. He particularly admired Brentry's 'most pleasing and extensive view. In the foreground are the rich woods of King's Weston and Blaize Castle, with the picturesque assemblage of gardens and villas in Henbury and Westbury; beyond which are the Severn and Bristol Channel, and the prospect is bounded by the mountains of South Wales.' He designed a drive which dramatised the burst of prospect which Brentry commands. He also laid out walks to the north of the house, and designed a grotto in the shrubbery to the south (Fig. 42).

The GROTTO at BRENTRY HILL BRISTOL _ Seat of W.ᵐ Payne Esq.ʳ

Fig. 42. Repton's grotto in the shrubbery at Brentry, from Peacock's Polite Repository, *1803.*

Between 1817 and 1825 an additional parcel of land was bought to the south, which allowed the road to be moved further from the house, along the line of the present Charlton Road. This fulfilled Repton's famous dictum on 'appropriation' – the art of giving the impression of 'unity and continuity of unmixed property'. The house was extended in the nineteenth century, but otherwise much of the landscape character remains.

The Royal Fort, Bristol – heaps and chasms
Another unusual commission was for the Royal Fort in Bristol, for which Repton produced a Red Book in 1801. The house, built in 1761 to a design by James Bridges, and park had been sold a few years earlier for speculative housing

development; however, the slump created by the Napoleonic Wars resulted in the estate reverting to the original owner. Colonel Thomas Tyndall called in Repton to see what he could do for this fine house, surrounded by the devastation of an abandoned building site. Repton wrote that when he arrived he found the house 'surrounded by vast chasms in the ground, and immense heaps of earth and broken rock'. With his usual practicality he turned the rubble and spoil to his advantage by constructing a large bank south of the house which allowed an unimpeded view from the house and garden over the city and beyond, while pedestrians passed by, unseen and unseeing, on the footpath below. The rest of the rubble and earth he used to create a pleasingly contoured garden around the house (Plates 20 and 21).

He did not try to shut out the surrounding city: 'few situations', he wrote in *Observations*, 'command so varied, so rich and so extensive a view as the Fort'. The garden was shaped and sculpted and was to have been planted up with shrubs and flowers. Although Tyndall's park has now been developed, the garden of the Royal Fort retains much of its historic character, while its value as a retreat from the surrounding city is greater than ever. It is now owned by Bristol University.

Ashton Court – ancient oaks and busy scenes

Repton had a hand in the design of the plantations in the old deer park at Ashton Court, which he visited in 1802. He seems to have been taken with the place, and made proposals for a new lake to the south of the house, which were not implemented, and designs for the plantations, which probably were. Repton was writing to the owner, Sir Hugh Smyth, in October 1802: 'I hope the ground I marked out for plantations has been prepared so as to be planted this season.' The extensive planting in 1803–4 – 10,000 trees were purchased from Miller & Sweet's nursery – and the sweeping drives are both Reptonian in style, and it seems likely that Smyth acted on his recommendations. Repton was particularly keen to make the most of views of the 'busy scene' of Bristol and the docks, rather than shut them out: it 'may appear objectionable to some, but I consider it among the most interesting circumstances belonging to the situation of Ashton Court', he wrote in *Observations* in 1803.

The beauty for which this fine park, now publicly owned, is so widely admired, stems from the brilliant planting of the early nineteenth century, which, sited and shaped to emphasise the natural contours of the land, lures the eye through the intervening lawns and glades.

Leigh Court and the staring yellow house

Late in his career Repton prepared a Red Book for a banker, Philip John Miles of Leigh Court in Abbot's Leigh. Here the earlier mansion was replaced in 1811 by a house designed by Thomas Hopper in the newly fashionable Greek Revival style. Repton had not been consulted about its location, and he criticised it in his text, in particular for its orientation towards a large yellow house in Abbot's Leigh – 'an obtrusive yellow mass of Ugliness', Repton snaps – over which Miles had no control (Plate 22).

Miles was one of the *nouveaux riches* for whom Repton was increasingly forced to work, but of whom he disapproved for their lack of the old Tory virtues of *noblesse oblige* and 'connection' with rural society. In 1816, he wrote: 'The sudden riches by individuals has diverted wealth into new chanels; men are solicitous to increase property rather than to enjoy it; they endeavour to impose the *value* rather than the *beauty* of their newly purchased estates.'

The most ambitious landscape feature – the drive – is not mentioned in the Red Book. However, it had been built within two years of Repton's visit, and the entrance lodge, built in the same severe style as the house, had been built by 1814. Fulfilling much the same dramatic function as the drive at Blaise, it may well have been proposed by Repton. The most picturesque part of Leigh Court was Paradise Bottom, the valley leading down to the river. Repton recommended making a path down to a rock seat, and this was done. He evidently also made a feature of some ancient small-leaved limes, and these are still in the valley. From the viewpoint, it was possible to see Cook's Folly, Blaise Castle, the Royal Fort, the Severn and the gorge.

Repton's other commissions

Repton is known to have visited a number of other sites in Avon. He prepared a Red Book for Newton Park, but it is thought that none of his main recommendations was implemented. He also worked at Dyrham, but on precisely what is not clear. He visited in 1800, and there are bills for payments of £66.3s in 1801 and £24.3s in 1803, as well as one sketch for 'the pavilion at the end of the terrace'. Most of the landscaping at Dyrham was being carried out by Charles Harcourt Masters, a surveyor from Bath.

Two other commissions for villa gardens like that at Brentry are known – Bailbrook House on the edge of Bath, and Cote Bank in Bristol – but details of the work are unclear. Of the latter, now demolished, Repton wrote in *Observations* that it was one of those sites 'where no house previously exists, and where the entire plan of the house, appendages, and grounds has sometimes been called a creation'. Bailbrook House had been built by 1791, and the owner who sought Repton's advice was a Mr Jones, but no Red Book is known to exist.

Regency Gardening – Sylva Florifera

W.S. Gilpin, nephew and pupil of the Reverend William, wrote that flowers were 'amenable to the rules of composition', and the art of the shrubbery developed on picturesque lines, with serpentine paths and island beds of mixed shrubs and flowers. *Sylva Florifera*, an influential textbook of 1823, by Henry Phillips, described this kind of planting.

Where space allowed, communal gardens were laid out on picturesque lines. The garden of Bellevue in Clifton, recorded on the 1828 Ashmead map of Bristol, shows winding walks through shrubberies, and irregular lawns (Fig. 43), in a style

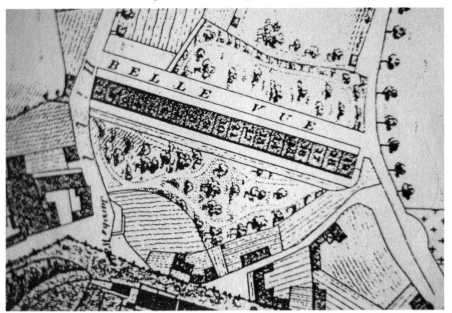

Fig. 43. Ashmead's 1828 map of Bristol, showing the picturesque communal garden below Bellevue.

that Repton and Nash pioneered in St James's Park in London, and which was soon being adapted for villa gardens in the suburbs.

Picturesque shrubberies afforded the planted framework to Bath's Sydney Gardens, created between 1793 and 1795 as a commercial pleasure garden. The gardens were crammed with ornaments and entertainments – painted tableaux, a 'Cosmorama' which showed Vesuvius erupting among other scenes, an aviary, a Chinese bridge, a pavilion, a ruined castle, a lake, a labyrinth 'twice as large as that in the gardens of Hampton Court', a grotto, swing boats, refreshments kiosks, and booths. There were dining boxes and orchestras, and at night, illuminations by over 15,000 lamps. So much incident was fitted into so small a site (recorded as 16 acres/6.5 hectares in 1825) by irregular beds of shrubs and trees dividing and screening the different compartments.

The late eighteenth and early nineteenth centuries saw an upsurge of interest in the arts of horticulture as distinct from landscape gardening. William Sole, a relation of Christopher Anstey and an apothecary of Bath, wrote an unpublished *Flora Bathonica* in 1782, while John Jelly, of the family of Bath builders, opened a Botanic Garden off Camden Road in 1793, in the 3/4-acre/0.3-hectare garden of his own house, Elm Bank. It seems to have been an attempt to capitalise on the public interest in botany:

> The Science of Botany is now so universally studied and admired; that to use any argument in favour of an institution like the present . . . would be altogether superfluous.

Jelly charged two annual subscription rates. Half a guinea entitled subscribers to walk in the garden, inspect the plants, and use a room and books provided; a guinea entitled them to 'receive roots and seeds of such plants as can be spared from the Garden to the full amount of their subscription and may introduce a Friend'. The venture was short-lived; in 1795 Jelly was declared bankrupt and his house, its contents and the garden with 'the moveable frames and stock of the Botanic Garden' were sold.

The greatest firm of Bristol nurserymen was Miller and Sweet, founded at the bottom of St Michael's Hill in 1785 by James Sweet who had been head gardener to Richard Bright at Ham Green. By 1822 the firm's Durdham Down nursery was the largest supplier in the south-west, from south Wales to Berkshire. Bills for Ashton Court from Miller and Sweet record the wealth of exotics planted in the first years of the nineteenth century: *Arbor vitae*, black and red American spruces, balsam poplar, American maples, cedar of Lebanon, acacias, laburnums and others. Other Bristol firms of the 1790s included Peter Lauder at Lawrence Hill and Edward Spiring of Upper Easton; William Maule's nursery, founded in the Stapleton Road in 1815, specialised in 'American Bog Plants', and a pretty cast-iron sign to Maule's later premises near Stoke Gifford still stands by the ring-road.

Bath was less well supplied with nurseries, a fact attributed by John Harvey to the temporary nature of aristocratic residence in the city, and to the ill-health that brought so many of its inhabitants to Bath. One family, the Salters, dominated trade in Bath between 1809 and 1850. They had nurseries at different times on Lyncombe Hill, by the London Road opposite Kensington Place, and on Weston Road near Royal Victoria Park, and linked to a town shop at 2 New Bond Street.

The passion for flowers had developed rapidly in the late eighteenth century, reflecting the increasing rate at which new species were being imported. In 1780, the Exeter nurseryman Joseph Ford was advertising in the *Bath Chronicle* not only 'a very curious collection of Persian Ranunculuses in full bloom, upwards of 10,000 in number' but also 'A curious collection of New Zealand Myrtles' and 'A variety of curious exotics from the South Seas'. Remarkably, this was only eleven years after Joseph Banks had sailed with Captain Cook on his first expedition to these places. In 1787, a Bath auctioneer advertised:

> A collection, consisting of near Two Hundred Pots of Myrtles and Geraniums, of the very best sort and handsome Growth; there are amongst them soe few curious Pots of Exotics . . . N.B.: As the above are the largest Number and greatest Variety that has been offered to public sale, they certainly claim the particular Attention of the curious in Green-House Plants.

At this date, a 'greenhouse' was used for plants requiring moderate heat only, whilst really tender specimens were kept in the better heated and rapidly developing range of 'conservatories' attached to the house. The remarkable series of paintings of the garden of 14 St James's Square in Bristol (Cover picture), attributed to a member of the Pole family who lived in the house, and dating from *c*.1805, show among many other fascinating features, a greenhouse in a modest-sized garden near the centre of the city. This building was heated by a stove, hence the chimney, the heat from which was conducted around the building by flues in the walls or under the floor. It is unlikely to have contained any hotbeds – pits containing bark or horse manure with a layer of soil on top, in which plants such as pineapples were planted to take advantage of the steady heat given off by the compost below – as these were mainly used for edible crops rather than the ornamental plants shown in the painting, and tended to require a lot of space. More than half St James's Square was destroyed by the Luftwaffe; the rest was razed by the City Council in the 1950s.

Abercrombie's *Gardener's Pocket Journal* (1806 edition) has instructions for greenhouses, and refers to over-wintering 'myrtles, geraniums, oleanders, as well as oranges, lemons and other exotics' before setting them out in pots in the garden. Another Pole painting shows an array of pots on a three-tier green-painted stand on the terrace by the house; a thermometer on the wall behind suggests these were exotics over which special care had to be taken.

'A View from Rauzzini's Garden in Bath', painted by William Capon in 1807 (Fig. 44), shows a pleasure ground embellished with numerous potted plants, while T.L.S. Rowbotham's painting of the garden front of Broomwell House, Brislington (*c.*1826), shows a great range of pots under the verandah flanking the garden door.

The Pole paintings and the Abercrombie handbook complement each other in a fascinating way. The extreme tidiness of the St James's Square garden is as

Fig. 44. 'View from the terrace of Signor Rauzzini's garden', painted by William Capon in 1807.

recommended in the handbook:

> All compartments – of borders, beds, shrubberies, lawns, walks, &c. keep
> in the neatest order, flower plants or irregular rude growth trim as required,
> and stick those wanting support; clip edgings and hedges; prune disorderly
> shrubs, &c. mow and sweep grass; weed, sweep and roll gravel.

The neatness of the beds is particularly strange to modern eyes, with plants widely
spaced as advised by Abercrombie: spacings of 6 inches/15 centimetres for small
bulbs, and 6–9 inches/15–22 centimetres for larger ones, 'in rows length wise', are
recommended. This style goes right back to the planting of specimen flowers in
the early seventeenth century.

The Regency period also saw the old 'rules of Taste' in architecture breaking
down. This was partly because of the new wealth of men without – or unshackled
by – a classical education; partly because of new influences – Chinese, Moorish,
'Hindoo' – resulting from Britain's expanding world trade; partly because of an
inevitable reaction against the straitjacket of Palladian (or Brownian) good taste;
and partly because of the shock to the *status quo* administered by the French
revolution, not helped by a mad king on the throne. Tim Mowl has identified a
picturesque 'painterly school of architecture' in this period – eclectic in style,
asymmetrical in design, and closely relating to the surrounding landscape.

The Regency itself lasted only from 1811 to 1820, but the Regent's succession
as king meant a continuity that lasted until his death in 1830, and with regard to
style, the word can be applied to the whole period.

Beckford's Ride

William Beckford, one of the most remarkable men of his day, possessor of one
of the most phenomenal private libraries ever collected, had a tower built on
Lansdown in what Pevsner has called a 'funereally Graeco-Egyptian style', to a
design by Henry Edmund Goodridge (Fig. 64). William Beckford – millionaire,
aesthete, collector, traveller, author – arrived in Bath in 1822, after selling his wildly
romantic Gothick house, Fonthill Abbey in Wiltshire, with its spire taller than
Salisbury Cathedral. He had created an enormous picturesque domain at Fonthill,
and behind his property on Lansdown Crescent he created a more modest but
equally original garden. This stretched up from the Crescent to the tower, and a
path ran through several distinct gardens. His gardener Vincent was instrumental
in the rapid development of this layout, transplanting sizeable trees with great
success.

Immediately behind Lansdown Crescent, four acres/1.6 hectares of the slope
were terraced with huge retaining walls and buttresses to form a sheltered fruit
garden. A huge battlemented gateway led from the terrace to pasture land which
Beckford planted up with thorns and clumps. The path then led up the hill to
various plantations, with rough-hewn seats from which to enjoy the prospects.
Past a cottage called the Bungalow, it proceeded through a low door in a wall into
a sunken walled garden some 400 feet/120 metres long and 80 feet/25 metres wide.

Then, through another arch, the path led past a pond to a long grotto tunnel, out across the down into a shrubbery, and past a rockery and ornamental pools to the tower.

Beckford died in 1844, and the estate was soon broken up and sold in small parcels of land. Much of it has been built over; the rear of Lansdown Crescent, Kingswood School and twentieth-century development further up the slope, such as Lansdown Park, have reduced Beckford's Ride to fragmentary remains. But immediately behind the Crescent the terraces and retaining walls of the fruit garden are still intact, as is the embattled gateway; the roof of his Turkish tea-house peeps over the walls of the garden of 20 Lansdown Crescent; traces of his planting and the walk survive in the grounds of the school; and the tunnel, although now blocked up, can still be seen. Beckford was buried by his tower, and the garden around the tower was made into a cemetery in 1848. Fortunately, Goodridge was still alive to design the perfectly funereal entrance gates.

Regency Gothick

Warleigh Manor

Warleigh Manor was built for Henry Skrine in 1815, in a picturesque Tudor Gothick style. This was also employed for the stable and outbuildings, and even the orangery was castellated. The slope from the house down to the Avon was formally terraced (Fig. 45); small bastions, stone retaining walls, flower beds and statuary created a quite formal garden in an old-fashioned style to match the architecture. In keeping with the time, however, a landscape park was created around the garden. Warleigh Manor is now a Special School, but the whole estate can be seen clearly from the footpath along the Kennet and Avon Canal on the opposite side of the Limpley Stoke Valley.

Banwell Caves – the bishop and the druids

The most unlikely Gothick garden was created by an eccentric churchman with antiquarian leanings. The Banwell Bone Cave had been discovered in 1824 by a local farmer, William Beard of Wint Hill. Its floor was covered with 'a huge mingled mass of bones and mud', including the remains of bison, cave lions, deer, bears, wolves, hyaenas and mammoths. The Cave quickly became a tourist attraction rivalling Cheddar, and the land around this and another large cave was soon bought by Dr Law, Bishop of Bath and Wells. He had a small *cottage orné* built on the site in 1827, which was later to become his permanent residence. Bishop Law, evidently fascinated by the caves, landscaped the site to create a place of both antiquarian interest and aesthetic pleasure, erecting a collection of follies which romantically evoked a prehistoric era. Law used revenue from the tourists to help fund a charity school in the village.

On top of the hill above the cottage, the bishop had a 'Neolithic Burial Chamber' built, and placed next to it a small Gothick summerhouse, decorated with flat pebbles on the walls and floor. From the burial chamber a walk led 600 yards/540

Fig. 45. The terraces at Warleigh Manor.

metres along the ridge to a tall Gothick prospect tower (Fig. 51). At intervals along the walk, 'Druidical' standing stones were placed in pairs. At the entrance to one of the caves, Law built a 'Druid's Temple', a recess behind three pointed arches, but the pagan theme was tempered here by a plaque which celebrated the light of Christianity banishing heathen darkness. The most spectacular building does not survive; this was an 'Osteoikon', for the exhibition of bones from the cave, which was thatched, with a façade richly decorated with spar and crystals. The whole garden was laid out with winding walks and shrubberies. It fell into neglect in the twentieth century and some of its buildings were destroyed. New owners are restoring it and the garden's structure is reappearing through the self-sown scrub.

Another intriguing Gothick folly of the early nineteenth century is Chota Castle at Chew Magna. The central castle building stands in a setting of rockeries, a pool, and lawns dotted with specimen trees.

Regency landscape gardens – Harptree Court and Brockley Hall

A compact picturesque layout was created at Harptree Court in East Harptree in the period *c.*1800 to 1820. Here, Charles Harcourt Masters demonstrated his skill as a landscape designer, laying out ornamental plantations around two lakes connected by a serpentine water course. An ice house and an elaborate grotto were also built, and survive intact. The park was ringed with a perimeter belt, and a lime and sweet chestnut avenue was planted. Within the garden, specimen trees were scattered across the lawn.

While Harptree Court survives in good condition, Brockley Hall at the foot of Brockley Combe has fared less well. The parkland close to the 1825 house has been built over with 1960s housing, while dilapidated caravans occupy the site of the glasshouses in the kitchen gardens, and the stables and coach house are abandoned ruins. But a grotto tunnel leading under Brockley Lane from the house to the kitchen gardens survives, its entrance flanked by stone sphinxes, and a single headless odalisque within (Fig. 46). Ashlar gate piers are surmounted by heraldic

Fig. 46. The entrance to the grotto at Brockley Hall.

beasts, and between them are elaborate wrought-iron gates. The undeveloped parkland is still an attractive sight from the A370, and best of all, the picturesque planting which was extended up into the Combe survives, and adds drama to the natural hanging woods.

The 1959 Department of the Environment listing reveals how much artificiality was not only tolerated but featured in the Regency garden. Apart from the sphinxes and heraldic beasts, it picks out for particular mention: stone Greek vases and pineapple urns along the coping of the walled garden; lead cupids; stone Greek heads; a semi-circular marble bench; a slender white marble seat divided by four couchant winged lions; a stone statue group in the centre of a circular pool, with a life-sized Poseidon; another group of the Three Graces.

Other picturesque or romantic landscapes of this period survive at Kingwell

Hall, Farmborough; Hollywood Tower, Almondsbury; Cleeve Court, Cleeve; and The Rocks at Marshfield.

The Development of Lansdown – catching the views

As Bath spread up the slopes of Lansdown, the steepest building sites became available just as the taste for panoramic views became fashionable. Camden Crescent, begun about 1788, occupies one of the most dramatic sites in the city; and indeed, it became an unintentionally picturesque sight itself when a landslip during building work caused the crescent to be cut short at its eastern end, leaving the ruined north-eastern pavilion perched on a rocky outcrop.

Lansdown Crescent was built *c.*1789–92, and despite the twentieth-century development on the other side of Bath, retains a spectacular prospect: in 1819, Pierce Egan described it as like 'looking down from the top of St Paul's Cathedral into the streets of London'.

The Picturesque also influenced the increasingly irregular layout of new development. St James's Square, for example, begun in 1790, was not square at all, and as all approaches entered on a diagonal from the corners of the rectangle, the view was directed straight into the garden. The Picturesque also resulted in such introductions (*c.*1794–1801) as the trees in the centre of the Circus.

With the end of the eighteenth century, or rather with the disastrous building crash of 1793, Bath's planned development was increasingly replaced by piecemeal suburban development. After the end of the Napoleonic wars, the well-off were tempted towards the fringes of the city, to detached villas in their own picturesque or gardenesque grounds.

Villa gardens

Henry Edmund Goodridge on Bathwick Hill – Florence in the west
Bath has a remarkable range of early nineteenth-century villa gardens. Uvedale Price had criticised Bath's architecture for its regularity imposed on such irregular ground: 'Whoever considers what are the forms of the summits, how little the buildings are made to yield to the ground, and how few trees are mixed with them, will account for my disappointment.' The response from Beckford's protégé Goodridge was a series of villas in an Italianate style, with highly irregular combinations of overhanging eaves, towers, loggias and balconies. The gardens combined formal and informal elements in a perfect match to the buildings.

The series on Bathwick Hill comprise Montebello (now called Bathwick Grange) which Goodridge built in 1828 for himself; Fiesole, which Goodridge moved into after he had sold Montebello; La Casetta; Casa Bianca; and Oakwood (then known as Smallcombe Grove) for Benjamin Barker the landscape painter known as 'the English Poussin'. In Bathwick Grange there are remains of the path system, with steps and a pond on the steep and wooded site, but the best survival of these Regency or William IV gardens is Oakwood.

Here, terraces outside the house and a walk along a shrub border by the wall to Bathwick Hill overlooked a dramatically sloping lawn and a chain of pools connected by cascades, over one of which a balustraded stone bridge was thrown. Through the garden trees the hanging woods of Smallcombe form the blue and misty background. There was a formal flower garden to the west of the house, but its real distinction was the picturesque lawn and ponds. The storm of 1990 brought down the cedars which formerly gave the lawns their mystery, and – a terrible intrusion – a large building has recently been allowed at the northern end of the chain of ponds. No longer does the garden descend into wildness, slanting 'Down the green hill athwart a cedarn cover', but since it was bought from the Salvation Army by an enthusiastic private owner there are great hopes of its revival and repair.

Vellore – General Augustus Andrews's 'consummable taste and judgement'
The villa, now the Bath Spa Hotel, was built in 1836 for General Augustus Andrews on his retirement from service in India. From then until his death in 1858, General Andrews spent a great deal on creating an elaborate villa garden. The house has subsequently been extended and remodelled, and one of the casualties was a conservatory, once said to have contained 2,000 exotic plants. In addition, the garden contained a fine collection of trees and shrubs.

According to the sale notice of 1858, the garden had been 'profusely adorned' with 'consummable taste and judgement' by the late owner. Within its six walled acres/2.6 hectares, it accommodated a Doric temple, which still faces a formal pond; a grotto in tufa said to have cost over £1,000; elaborate shrubberies; serpentine paths; another pool; a rustic summerhouse; terraces; parterre flower beds; steps; statuary; and stonework. 'In the summer', according to the sale notice, 'the Gardens are a complete Rosary as there are nearly 200 distinct varieties of this beautiful flower'.

Small and intensively ornamented, with a stress on the display of exotics, it is a fine example of an early nineteenth-century villa garden in a very different style from the English Poussin's picturesque layout.

Cote – a Bristol villa
Bristol's suburbs were also expanding in the nineteenth century. An example of a villa garden from this period is Cote at Westbury-on-Trym. This was the Bristol home of the Wedgwood family, rich and influential dissenters, whose fortune had been made by Josiah senior in his pottery works at Etruria. Two of his three sons, the second and third, Thomas and Josiah, were generous patrons of the new intellectual movement of the 1790s, friends of Mary Wollstonecraft and William Godwin, of Humphry Davy, and of Wordsworth and Coleridge. Tom Wedgwood in particular was a romantic figure – an experimenter in everything from photography to hallucinogenic drugs.

The first Wedgwood son, John, was a banker and a distinguished amateur horticulturist. With Sir Joseph Banks, he formed the Horticultural Society of London in 1804, which later became the Royal Horticultural Society. He moved from London to Cote in 1797, where he grew a wide range of flowers, azaleas, tulips and carnations as well as exotic fruit in the glasshouses and walled gardens. Business difficulties forced him to sell Cote in 1806, and it is uncertain how much of the present layout is his. The orangery is eighteenth-century, and the terraced lawns and walk may well be the same on which Coleridge, Davy and Tom Wedgwood walked and talked, while the unique keyhole-shaped walled garden in the grounds of the neighbouring Badminton School is also thought to have been part of Wedgwood's complex.

The estate was owned by the Ames family from 1806 until 1923, and much of the surviving exotic planting and ornament, including the Pulhamite rock work, derives from them in the picturesque style of the 1830s. The gardens at Cote are now partly built over, and the house was demolished and replaced with St Monica's Home in 1925.

Fromeshaw House and Lake House – a Regency miniature
On the edge of Frenchay Common, a miniature Regency landscape was laid out for Fromeshaw House, now divided into two dwellings – Fromeshaw House and Lake House – adapting what appears to have been an older building and its grounds. The garden was approached via steps from a terrace, at one end of which is a tiny Gothick grotto, still in part lined with shells and spars, and little bigger than a telephone box. On one side of the lawn stand the remains of a small chapel-like garden building and the remains of glasshouses. The lawn, dotted with specimen cedars and Scots pine, slopes down to a 1/2-acre/0.2-hectare lake, containing an island reached by a bridge. The dovecote is now the Electricity Sub-station.

Chapter 5

Victorian and Edwardian Parks and Gardens

VICTORIAN GARDENS came in all shapes and sizes. Unlike earlier periods, no particular style predominated because their number, variety, location and use became legion. What was right for an extensive landscape park could hardly be applied to the thousands of suburban gardens that sprang up in the wake of the massive urbanisation that accompanied the industrial revolution; what was right for a public park was not for a small town garden. New influences came to bear – technological, social and economic – which helped to emphasise gardening skills rather than the large-scale redesigning of landscape which had gone before.

The period witnessed not only the culmination of the country house style but also the evolution of gardening principles applicable to smaller country houses, to suburban villas, and to town gardens. It was also the golden age of social concern, and this too was expressed in gardening. New demands for social provision required new design solutions in the laying out of public parks, garden cemeteries and institutional landscapes.

The different manifestations of the gardener's art did, however, have key, distinctively Victorian, features in common. The mania for collecting plants was fuelled by plant-finding expeditions to far-flung parts of the world, newly opened up for trade. This was the period when the plant collectors hit the jackpot, when, in addition to wonderful discoveries in west-coast America, Asia began to yield her secrets. Many of our most valued garden plants were brought to England during Victoria's reign – the Hooker rhododendrons (1847), for example, and the conifers of the west coast of North and South America. The wealth of new plants soon gave rise to the collectors' gardens – the arboretum, the pinetum and the botanic garden – and nurseries expanded and proliferated to satisfy the demand for the latest introductions.

The obsession with plants of all kinds, the weirder the better, demanded of the gardener new skills and facilities for their care, propagation and hybridisation. Alpines required rock and scree gardens; ferns demanded shady humidity; and half-hardy or frost tender plants needed protection from the cold. The Victorians became masters at providing the conditions in which plants were able to thrive, through a combination of green-thumbed perseverance, horticultural expertise and the application of technological fixes. This was the era of hothouses and ferneries, of palm courts and winter gardens, of pineapple pits and banana houses, of fresh strawberries served at Christmas dinner.

The bedding out of half-hardy plants, changed twice or even three times a year, became the norm in all Victorian gardens, from grand country houses (using perhaps 20,000 scarlet geraniums in one display), municipal parks and strand walks, to the front gardens of urban dwellers.

The use of so many new plants led to more space being dedicated to their cultivation. This brought about the construction of more and bigger walled gardens, with heated walls and acres of glasshouses and frames. The orangeries of the eighteenth century gave way to conservatories, perfect for the care and exhibiton of exotic plants. The passion for massive outdoor displays encouraged the revival of the fashion for elaborate parterres close to the house. Distinct garden areas, divided from each other by clipped hedges or walls, and long-since unfashionable, also made a comeback, allowing plants to be shown to their best advantage.

Gardening Style – 'wild' versus formal

Towards the end of the century, arguments about how best to display plants led to two recognisable styles of gardening: the plantsman's or 'wild' garden, as advocated by William Robinson, garden writer and magazine editor, and the formal garden as advocated by Reginald Blomfield, architect and garden designer, in his *The Formal Garden In England* (1892). The first extolled the virtues of herbaceous borders, rock gardens and woodland gardens; the other bitterly attacked naturalistic gardening, advocating instead an architectural approach to design. Blomfield's view was that Capability Brown 'took the judicious line that knowledge hampered originality. He accordingly dispensed with any training in design, and rapidly rose to eminence'. In his book Blomfield reproduced Kip engravings, showing the formal William and Mary layouts which, as Celia Fiennes put it, combined 'ornament, pleasure and use'.

Robinson's immensely influential book, *The English Flower Garden* (1883), advocates, on the other hand, the kind of garden like that of his friend, Canon Ellacombe at Bitton:

> a quiet, peaceful garden of grass and trees and simple borders and every nook and corner has its appropriate flower, in a word, it is just such a garden as one would expect a scholar to possess who has sympathy for all that lives and breathes.

Resolving the conflict – Gertrude Jekyll and Harold Peto

It was the great achievement of Edwardian gardeners like Gertrude Jekyll and Harold Peto that they succeeded in harmonising the apparently conflicting traditions of plantsmanship and architectural layout. Jekyll, a friend of Robinson and Ellacombe, was a painter, garden designer and prolific writer. In an article entitled 'Changes of Fashion in Gardening', published in 1928, she acknowledged Canon Ellacombe as 'a grower of a wide range of garden plants who gave willing and most precious help to the many needing better knowledge'.

Gertrude Jekyll's greatest gardens were those that she designed in partnership with Edwin Lutyens. These united firm architectural lines with lavish and varied planting often inspired by traditional cottage gardens. Gardens designed by Jekyll and Lutyens, like those of the seventeenth century, were often divided into a series of outdoor rooms, with each compartment being as different one from another as ingenuity and good taste would allow. But Miss Jekyll was one of the first to use a wide range of plants in an association of masses, producing distinctive colour effects. From the glowing hot orange and reds of poppy and kniphofia, to the silver and whites of senecio and cerastium, she selected the colours from the artist's palette to create the impression of a painting filling and overflowing each outdoor room. Jekyll did not work in Avon (although she did nearby at Hestercombe and elsewhere in Somerset), but her books and her ideas were a major influence in changing the nature of English gardening in the twentieth century.

Landscape Parks – business as usual

Throughout the first third of the nineteenth century the influence of the eighteenth-century tradition of gardening remained dominant, and new parks were still being laid out or 'improved' in largely informal styles. Even after gardening fashion changed in favour of smaller, more intimate designs, landscape parks were still in demand as symbols of status and influence.

In Avon, the last of the type were at Eastwood for Lord Liverpool, Tyntesfield for William Gibbs (later Lord Wraxall) and Tortworth for the Earl of Ducie, all laid out from the 1840s and improved throughout the century. Although similar to eighteenth-century designs in their structure and grandeur, these late parks also exhibited the Victorian obsession with plants in the development of extensive arboreta specialising in exotics and new introductions. Ashwicke Hall, near Marshfield, was perhaps the last true landscape park in the county. Begun in 1860 and remodelled from 1900 to 1920, Ashwicke contains all the features associated with traditional country seats: walled gardens, stables, lake, avenues, well-timbered parkland and woodland.

Tortworth Park

Tortworth Park is of particular interest in its combination of eighteenth-century Brownian style and Victorian innovations. An extravagant Gothic house, designed by Samuel Teulon, was built in 1849–50 on the brow of a hill commanding extensive

Fig. 47. Tortworth Court and lake from a postcard of c. 1910

views of the rolling landscape. An artificial lake was created by damming a small stream, and this was decorated with a boathouse and dense bankside planting of dark conifers, producing an effect evocative of alpine scenery (Fig. 47). Terraced formal gardens and shrubberies were laid out around the house and 21 acres/8 hectares were devoted to an arboretum.

Tortworth now contains one of the most outstanding private collections of trees in the country, and one of the best documented. Begun in the 1850s by the 3rd Earl of Ducie, the arboretum is well known for its fine specimens of east American oaks, hickories and maples. The Earl's love of recently imported conifers gives Tortworth an unusual and exotic appearance and character. Ducie was a friend of the Holfords of Westonbirt, who shared his interest in trees and shrubs with good autumn colour. Of course Westonbirt's subsequent history makes it better known today, but in their formative stages the two collections grew as a result of collaboration and friendly competition, so that many new acquisitions were simultaneous. In the early 1900s both gardens were commended for their collections of trees and shrubs with autumnal tints by the leading nurseryman Mr Harry Veitch, who no doubt supplied many of the plants he so admired.

As well as the usual sources of cuttings and seeds from friends, the Tortworth arboretum was stocked from a number of nurseries. Examples from the estate account books include:

20/6/1850 to Mr Knight and Perry, Garden Seeds etc £23/2/0. [This was the Exotic Nursery in King's Road, Chelsea which was known for its stocks of hardy ornamental trees and shrubs and American plants.]

7/1/1850 to Garaway, Mayes & Co. £5/9/0.
3/3/1851 to Mr Gregory for taking up and packing shrubs purchased at his sale [at Cirencester] by Mr Stephens £4/3/0.
13/3/1851 to Mr Gregory for taking up and packing shrubs purchased at his sale Nov 1852 Mr Crumb's [Head Gardener] Expenses to London £3/0/0.
5/12/1854 Messrs Maule & Sons £25/10/0.
29/1/1856 Mr James Veitch Jnr. £73/3/6.
12/5/1860 Mr Wheeler [the leading Gloucester nursery] for Lawn Grass etc. £7/7/0.

Tockington Manor
Not far from Tortworth is the Tockington Manor arboretum, with many varieties of oak and cedars, including a rare golden cedar, said to be one of only six in this country. This collection of trees is probably about a hundred years old. At that time the manor house, now a school, was owned by Captain Thomas Salmon, who brought back saplings from his seafaring. This arboretum is currently being augmented under the guidance of Alan Mitchell. The school grounds may be visited during the Open Village Week each year.

Ashton Court and Leigh Court
The availability of exotic trees not only influenced the design of new landscapes such as Tortworth and Tyntesfield, but also changed the character and appearance

Fig. 48. Leigh Court depicted in a lithograph by T.S. Butterworth of c.1830.

of established landscape parks, notably Ashton Court and Leigh Court (Fig. 48). At both places a renewed wave of planting of new introductions followed remodelling by Humphry Repton. In the 1850s the Ashton Court estate was inherited by Sir Greville Smyth who added cedars and sequoias in avenues, and as specimens in the formal garden, in 1866. The latter are said to have been the first planted from seed in this region. The parkland still boasts many mixed plantations from the period, although the restoration plan carried out by Bristol City Council and Task Force Trees (set up by the Countryside Commission after the storms of 1987) in 1992 identified the loss of hundreds of single conifer specimens.

Ashton Court was also noted for other typical late Victorian garden features: a winter garden packed with luxurious tropical plants, and a rockery which housed the alpine collection. The winter garden became unsafe and was dismantled and stored in 1974, but the rockery was replanted in 1982. Two Gothic lodges were added in the 1880s: Clifton Lodge after the opening of Clifton Suspension Bridge, and Church Road Lodge.

Clevedon Court
At Clevedon Court (Fig. 49), the woods behind the house were extended and interplanted throughout the nineteenth century, culminating in Mary Stewart's (Lady Elton's) accomplished redesign of the 1850s (Fig. 50). She introduced a great deal of exotic planting into an extensive layout of wood walks that commanded

Fig.49. A pencil drawing of Clevedon Court by Lady Elton, 1824.

Fig. 50. Lady Mary's Wood walks at Clevedon Court photographed by W.H. Barton c.1880.

wide prospects of the surrounding landscape, including the picturesque valley known as Little Switzerland.

In her *Wall and Water Gardens* (1901) Gertrude Jekyll recognised the quality of this site, but was scathing about the Victorian garden planting:

> The planting at the base of the lowest wall seems in these more horticulturally enlightened days to be quite indefensible. The foot of one of the noblest ranges of terrace walls in England is too good to be given over to the most commonplace forms of bedding . . .

It is indicative of the changing fashion in garden design that only a couple of years earlier the beds that she referred to, set square against the wall, had been praised lavishly in *Country Life* magazine. Victorian photographs show the area directly behind the house set out as an elaborate parterre; this was first planted in 1857 and removed a century later. Over recent years the gardens have been replanted by the present Lady Elton and the National Trust with a softer combination of shrubs and plants. Designed as they are to combine subtle colours and foliage effects, they might well have appealed to Miss Jekyll.

Newton Park

Newton Park (Plate 23) also shows the effect of the Victorian passion for new trees and shrubs. Extensively landscaped by Capability Brown in the eighteenth century, and refined by Repton, Newton Park was embellished in Victorian times with sequoias, monkey puzzles, cedars and other conifers. Among the account books of the 1860s for Newton Park are bills from Maule and Son and Joseph Dublin, nurserymen, and, in 1877, a payment of £24/3/8 to Masters Stothert and Pitt, Bath ironfounders, for a new conservatory.

Smaller Country Houses – in imitation of the past

In many ways the Victorians were backward-looking in their tastes. This was the era not only of the 'restoration' of older houses in historic idiom – often involving a complete rebuild – but of new solidly built Courts, Granges, Halls and Villas, whose revivalist designs drew on Tudor, Jacobean and vernacular architecture with their French, Italian and Dutch influences. All reflected an idealised re-creation of history, and all demanded appropriate settings. Only rarely, where money allowed and the fancy struck, was a more ambitious structure raised. In 1848 John Dyer Simpson erected Banwell Castle, an elaborate sham furnished with battlemented gardens and terraces within a castle wall with towers and turrets (Fig. 51). Gardens

Fig. 51. The Gothick tower at Banwell Castle.

became as eclectic as the buildings, encompassing Japanese tea gardens, herbaceous borders, and Tudor knots, often on the same site.

Formal architectural gardens, their layout extending from the lines of the house, fitted the nostalgic mood, and had the advantage of providing a wide range of conditions for growing plants. By the 1880s elaborate and complex geometric gardens were again being laid out in this country.

Barrow Court

The best example locally is at Barrow Court, laid out between 1892 and 1896 by F. Inigo Thomas, a collaborator of Blomfield in advocating a return to formal styles. The garden was carefully subdivided by large tightly clipped yew hedges to create separate 'outdoor rooms'; these were richly ornamented with statues, ponds, summerhouses, loggias and other garden buildings, and avenues of fruit trees in the kitchen garden were trained to match the yew hedges. The garden had a maze at its centre, with balanced herb and rose gardens on either side. Even that typically Victorian feature, the ubiquitous shrubbery, at one side of the garden, was formally laid out. Carefully trimmed avenues gave clear views of distant ornaments at the far end of the garden; here the lawn terminated in a high railing and gates in a half-circle, with the 'terms' or twelve months of the year represented by the sculpted heads of women, ageing in stages from baby to elder. Infinite care was taken over every aspect of the garden's composition, and the result was a masterpiece.

Fig. 52. Barrow Court; a photograph of the 1960s.

Although now in divided ownership, the garden at Barrow Court has survived in comparatively good condition (Fig. 52 and Plate 24).

Thornbury Castle

Perhaps the most impressive of the county's Victorian restorations was at Thornbury Castle, where Anthony Salvin transformed the largely ruinous buildings into a family home, incorporating vestiges of the sixteenth-century courts and privy gardens with their bee-boles and geometric beds (Plate 40).

Clevedon Hall and others

The prevailing character of mid- to late-Victorian layouts is also typified by the Jacobean revival Clevedon Hall (until recently St Brandon's School) with its statues, fountain, formal flower beds and dark, evergreen shrubberies; by Stanshawe's Court, Yate, with its crinkle-crankle wall; or by the vicarage garden at The Knoll, Clevedon. Perhaps the most fascinating example of history in miniature is at Lilliput Court, Yate, where the architecture appears to be half-scale and all the features in the 10-acre/4-hectare park are of diminutive proportions. The garden and park are separated by a ha-ha so low that one wonders if anything larger than a guinea pig ever grazed there.

Iford Manor

Like Gertrude Jekyll, Harold Peto, architect and garden designer, believed that to achieve the greatest beauty, a garden must be a combination of artefacts and plants, with hard and soft elements in harmony. He was particularly influenced by Italian gardens, producing his finest work on steep slopes where he could dramatise the changes of level with steps, terraces and planting.

Iford Manor (Plate 25), Peto's home from 1901, stands just above the River Frome on the Avon and Wiltshire border. A dizzyingly steep staircase beside the house leads up to the main garden with lead urns, statues on pillars, columnar cypresses and a large yew all contributing to the Italianate impression. Between each flight of steps is a small terrace, each one of a different design, with careful planting chosen for colour and foliage effects. The main terrace at the top of the garden is an architectural and scenic triumph, with horticulture playing an important but subordinate role. Enclosed by columns, it consists of a gravel promenade edged with paving. The walk leads from an octagonal eighteenth-century garden house at the east end to an open view of the sky framed by columns above a semicircular seat and a well-head at the other. Repeated plantings of Italian cypress, phillyrea, juniper, box and yew are used to add dramatic deep shadows and contrasts of form to the distant views.

From the eastern end of the terrace a path leads past massive sweet chestnut trees and across an open bulb-planted meadow to the Cloisters, an Italian Romanesque building designed by Peto to make use of the remainder of the ancient fragments he had collected from Italy. The atrium provides superb views both outwards over the valley from the little balcony and backwards to the house. Higher up is a woodland garden, and against the hill a little Japanese garden containing bamboos, tree peonies, cherries and a hardy palm.

Widcombe Manor and Barley Wood

Part of the garden of Widcombe Manor (Plate 36), where the structure of the early eighteenth-century garden survives, was also given the Italianate treatment early in the twentieth century. The reworking has been attributed to Peto on stylistic grounds, as have the Edwardian gardens at Barley Wood, laid out for H.H. Wills from 1901 to 1911 in a larger informal park landscaped for Hannah More in 1801. Here an elaborate walled and terraced kitchen garden was made to balance a terraced ornamental garden, with large tightly clipped yew hedges a prominent feature of both. The kitchen garden was subdivided geometrically with gravel paths bordered by low box hedges.

Crowe Hall – an informal 'villa garden'

One of the best examples of the large 'villa garden', harking back to Italian models in a more informal way, was developed at Crowe Hall (Plate 27), above Widcombe village. On a site dating back to 1760, a garden rich in detail and inspiration was developed throughout the nineteenth century. It evolved, by the 1880s, into an Italianate terrace and formal beds and lawn near the house, linked by paths through rockwork and a grotto to a wilderness below. The Italophile owner was Henry Tugwell, whose head gardener was William Carmichael, a Scot trained at the Edinburgh Botanic Gardens, and who had been head gardener to the Prince of Wales at Sandringham in the 1860s. His azalea 'William Carmichael' was awarded a first-class certificate by the Royal Horticultural Society in 1878.

The great, if cheeky, inspiration was to use the mansion of Prior Park as a distant eyecatcher, as if it were just a garden building erected to enhance the view.

More Victorian revivals

Avon contains numerous historic properties that were given a facelift by the Victorians. Typical examples are Churchill Court, Langford Court and Nailsea Court. At St Catherine's Court (Fig. 53), the early seventeenth-century terrace garden was given new 'Jacobean' balustrades with stone vases and finials, a bowling green and an impressive grass stairway connecting the walks on different levels. A terraced walk behind crenellated 'fortifications' was added to the layout at Lyegrove House, with a woodland wilderness and a new avenue. Ventilators for the railway tunnel were built in the form of Gothic towers at Lyegrove and Badminton, at the insistence of the Beauforts and other powerful Gloucestershire families.

Southmead Manor and Holmwood – combining the formal and the naturalistic

Two notable gardens, both close to Bristol, which exemplify a typical turn-of-the-century combination of formal and naturalistic elements, were made by Dr Stanley

Fig. 53. St Catherine's Court in a postcard of c.1915.

Badock at Southmead Manor and Holmwood in Westbury-on-Trym. Southmead Manor was a rebuilt seventeenth-century house, but many of the earlier garden features were retained, including a ruined gazebo. Holmwood was a new house, and had a garden designed in the Arts and Crafts style, overlooking a steep valley. The garden at Holmwood was the forerunner of the type of garden which, in diluted form, is associated with 1930s bungalows and semis: a sunken rose garden and pool surrounded with paving; rustic wood trellises and a pergola.

Both Southmead and Holmwood had 'wild' gardens laid out along small streams, as well as extensive plantings of specimen trees. The two gardens were linked by Badock's ambitious ornamental landscaping and planting scheme along the River Trym, where an artificial pool survives as Henleaze Lake. Badock's Wood also survives, in a somewhat sad condition, as public open space.

Gardens for Plants

Winscombe Hall

In 1858, a garden was made at Winscombe Hall for the Reverend John Augustus Yatman. It featured a Tudor summerhouse and various historic architectural knick-knacks, including the ruins of the earlier house, and was stocked by far-flung members of the family. The Reverend Yatman and his brother collected in Europe; his brother-in-law settled in Australia; and his eldest son spent six months of every year in New Zealand. All contributed plants to the garden.

Whiteshill House

In the Edwardian period the wild woodland garden, often associated with water, became an accepted element for areas farthest from the house, with, nearer the

VIEW FROM THE FORT, NEAR BRISTOL.

VIEW FROM THE FORT, NEAR BRISTOL.

Plates 20 and 21. Repton's before and after illustrations from the Red Book for the Royal Fort estate in Bristol.

Plate 22. The yellow house at Leigh Court from Repton's Red Book.

Plate 23. The landscape park at Newton Park – designed by Capability Brown and refined by Humphry Repton.

Plate 24. The triumph of the architectural garden – Barrow Court, designed by F. Inigo Thomas between 1892 and 1896.

Plate 25. Iford Manor – Harold Peto's Italian fantasy set in the English countryside.

Plate 26. The rock garden at Rayne Thatch, on the very edge of Clifton gorge.

Plate 27. Crowe Hall, on the northern side of Bath, commands marvellous views towards Prior Park.

Plate 28. The Japanese garden at Oaklands depicted in a nineteenth-century watercolour by an unknown artist.

Plate 29. Eastville Park dates from the heyday of public parks in the late nineteenth century.

Plate 30. The Winter Gardens at Weston-super-Mare.

Plate 31. In Royal Victoria Park in Bath a cheerful nineteenth-century atmosphere is skilfully maintained.

house, semi-formal arrangements of paving, walls with raised beds, and walks and steps, all providing a variety of niches for specialised plants.

The gardens around Whiteshill House in Hambrook beautifully exemplified this style. A famous showpiece before World War II, Whiteshill was begun by Dr Francis Crossman in 1904. In its heyday it boasted terraces and dry-stone walls crammed with alpines, while a complicated system of pools and rocks were laid out alongside steps down to a valley garden straddling Bradley Brook. This deeply enfolded woodland garden contained a mixture of 'Pacific' plants from California, as well as specimens from China and Japan. Beneath a towering canopy of giant sequoias there were rhododendrons, acacias and bamboos, and the whole site was studded with a vast collection of spring-flowering bulbs. The neglected condition of what survives only adds to the garden's romance and one's delight in the unexpected discovery of tiny nodding reflexed narcissi or snowdrops in the rough grass and leaf-litter.

Fashionable trees

Almost all the minor country seats in the county saw the addition of some of the newly fashionable trees. At Cleeve Court near Brockley the woodland was interplanted with exotic conifers and mixed shrubs, many of which survive. At Doynton House a collection of exotic trees was added to the seventeenth-century grounds, and specimen trees were added to the garden at Hinton House, Hinton Charterhouse. Wellingtonias grown from seed brought back on the SS *Great Britain* mingle with monkey puzzle trees at Marlwood Grange in Thornbury. Most pre-existing layouts had shrubberies and woodland walks added to them to bring them up to date.

At Eagle House in Batheaston an arboretum was established in the early twentieth century, where each tree commemorated a suffragette imprisoned for her cause. This site has since been completely destroyed.

Suburban Gardens – the search for privacy

Some of the smaller country houses are now in suburbia, swallowed up by the rapid expansion of towns and cities during the nineteenth century. By 1851, for the first time, more people in Britain were living in towns than in the country. Massive urban migration of impoverished farm workers, coupled with a population explosion, meant that urban areas witnessed unprecedented rates of growth. Suburban development was quickly transformed from the building of single houses to the creation of hundreds of houses in new residential areas. The first suburban houses were rapidly engulfed by hordes of others, all seeking space, privacy and seclusion.

There are many examples of once spacious villa gardens carved up for more intensive development. Cranwells at New Weston, built in 1850, was an estate of 30 acres/12 hectares, now subdivided, and with only some fine trees remaining to hint at the former glory of the garden. The Villa Rosa in Weston-super-Mare was built in 1847 but its land had already been built over by 1859, leaving only fragments of lawn and trees now cared for by the local authority.

Loudon and the 'Gardener's Magazine'

In 1826, J.C. Loudon, the influential writer, editor and landscape gardener, founded the *Gardener's Magazine*, which was to guide the development of new styles of gardening for suburban dwellers, and recommend plants to go with them. New exotics were pouring into the country from all over the world, and even people with only a small plot to tend wanted to know about and to grow them. The Chilean pine, or monkey puzzle, was one of the intriguing introductions of the period; the sight of one of these trees today in a nineteenth-century street testifies to the passion of some long-dead gardener. Loudon believed that foreign trees and shrubs were essential for 'good taste' in gardening. In 1838 he wrote: 'The grounds of every country seat, from the cottage to the mansion, will become an arboretum, differing only in the number of species which it contains.'

'Good taste' gardening

Gardens varied, of course, according to the enthusiasm, space, time and money available, but a distinct style did nevertheless evolve in the nineteenth century. Geometrical flower beds were often placed close to the house, with a patio or sometimes a conservatory making a transition from house to garden. Beyond these flower beds an irregularly shaped lawn, with more beds, trees and shrubberies, helped to break up straight lines and suggest a certain natural evolution of the garden. Often, classical or rustic stone urns or statues were set up, and seats strategically placed for the perambulation along gravel or stone paths and steps. Exotic plants were a necessity: yuccas, japonicas, peonies, alpines, bamboos and many others, bringing colour, variety and novelty to the garden.

Alpines and rockwork

Alpines became a passion, as English visitors to the Alps learned to combine mountaineering with plant collecting. Rockeries had been used before, but it was in the nineteenth century that they became a commonplace element of good gardening, and were often combined with a water garden – making it possible to grow specialised aquatic plants. Where natural rock was difficult or expensive to obtain, artificial rock, known as Pulhamite, produced by Pulham & Son of London (1830–1945), was often used.

The Wills family, tobacco barons, played a prominent part in garden layout in and around Bristol in the nineteenth and early twentieth centuries (members of the family still have interesting gardens today in Avon and Gloucestershire). In the early part of the twentieth century Pulham worked for Melville Wills at his home, Brackenwood, and at Rayne Thatch (Plate 26), the estate office nearby. At Rayne Thatch, lying above Nightingale Valley and the Avon Gorge, elaborate rockwork was constructed to form great pools and cascades; the water was circulated by a pump housed in a Gothic Pulhamite pump house. The longest pool was designed and used as a swimming pool, and a bridge led across to a party room above the offices. The garden was decked with coloured fairy lights and lanterns. At Brackenwood, the gardens and exuberant rockeries have been conserved as part of the Botanic Gardens for Bristol University. Alpine collections have flourished among the rockwork, but these are now under threat from the University's development aspirations.

Towards the end of the nineteenth century, the Wills family made the dramatically sited terrace garden at Burwalls, on the Leigh Woods side of Clifton Suspension Bridge, which included an Iron Age hill fort in its design; and extensive use was again made of Pulhamite at the Bristol Homeopathic Hospital which they built in 1926–7.

Hothouses and conservatories

The removal of the tax on window glass, advances in metal-working technology, and the development of steam or hot water heating, soon led to a craze for hothouses and conservatories. These became an essential part of even the smallest Victorian houses, providing a sheltered environment for growing tender and half-hardy exotics.

Few suburban gardens of the nineteenth century survive in any state of completeness. Many have been subdivided for further building plots; others have been paved to provide a space for the family car; most have been reworked and replanted several times by successive owners, so that trees and shrubs are often the only surviving elements of the original layout. Where remnants do survive, the Avon Gardens Trust has been active in seeking their preservation or restoration. For example, the early greenhouse at Linden, in Weston on the edge of Bath, was saved from demolition and is to be restored by the present owners of the hotel as an amenity for guests.

Plant Collecting and Garden Introductions

The vast majority of plants grown in English gardens today are of exotic origin. The excitement and adventure, as well as the scientific interest, that their collection involved, were matched at home by the enthusiasm of botanists and gardeners to grow them, study them and develop new hybrids from them. The introduction of the Wardian case in the late 1830s meant that plants which had previously been known only as dried specimens in herbaria could survive long sea voyages to Britain, while improved communications, canals and particularly railways, meant plants could be despatched more easily internally. As a result, the number of nurseries increased dramatically, and printed catalogues enabled them to widen their markets.

Popular horticultural journals became hugely successful, and horticultural societies sprang up everywhere. The Bath and West of England Society was founded in 1800, with the Bristol nurseryman Nehemiah Bartley as secretary. Bartley was not an administrative success, but the Society flourished and horticultural exhibitions became a popular attraction. The Bristol Botanical and Horticultural Society was formed in 1830.

The passion for collecting is well illustrated in an account of an expedition undertaken by two plantsmen and gardeners from Avon. Hiatt Baker (of Oaklands in Almondsbury) describes the expedition to the Alps that he made in 1903 with Canon Ellacombe of Bitton. Canon Ellacombe, well known as a plant collector and gardener, was then eighty-one years old.

> Canon Ellacombe had always had a fancy to go over the Muscera Pass from Simplon to Domodossola; it seems some ancient writer had said that it was very rich in flowers; and having been on three occasions baulked by adverse circumstances, he asked Lascelles and me to see him over it . . . We started at about 6 o'clock and all went well over the first pass, but having got down into the next valley our route was by no means certain. We pushed on through deepish snow to the top of the next ridge, and on the other side we got into a tangle of torrents running through boulders and rhododendron scrub, and to add to our difficulties it thundered and rained for all it was worth. The Canon was quite placid, sitting on his horse as if he were part of it (it was as often as not on its head or its knees!), a huge white cotton umbrella over his head, and continually shouting 'Baker! Baker! What's that flower?' I may say the water was streaming down my backbone!
>
> He was not much moved when our so-called guide, casting his staff from him, fell on his knees in prayer (one does not altogether like one's temporal guide to turn in obvious despair to spiritual resources!). I was beginning to be really alarmed, afraid that at any moment he might come down and break his bones. Finally we got to a place where we could not possibly get the horses down; what we should have done if some charcoal burners had not come to our rescue, I don't know.

Landowners competed to acquire these new introductions, and the gardens of Avon still bear the fruits of such plant-collecting expeditions.

Botanic Gardens

In Bristol, plans were launched for zoological and botanical gardens on Durdham Down. The grounds were landscaped by Richard Forrest of Miller's Durdham Down Nurseries, and the site was officially opened in 1836 (Fig. 54). Many specimen trees were planted, including cedars grown from seed. It soon became obvious that it was too much for the management committee to run both the zoological and botanical collections, so the gardens at the zoo were taken over by Miller's nursery and maintained by them for some years. In the second half of the century, the zoo had the largest local collection of hollies and the finest collection of ferns in the British Isles. The ferns were assembled by Edwin Fydell Fox, fern collector and hybridiser, and son of Edward Long Fox of Brislington House.

In Bath, Sir Jerom Murch is a name famous in the world of plants. He built

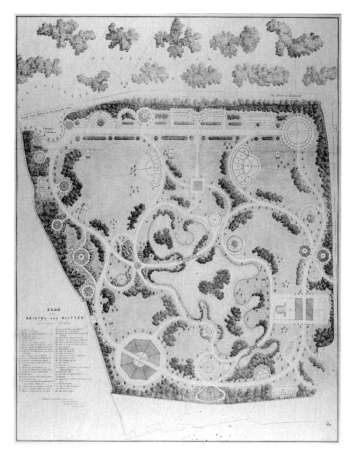

Fig. 54. Richard Forrest's design for Bristol and Clifton Zoological Gardens. Lithograph c.1840.

his house Cranwells at New Weston in the 1850s, and stocked the garden with an extensive collection of conifers, some of which remain. He also laid out the north-west corner of Royal Victoria Park at his own expense, and was Mayor of Bath when the City accepted the posthumous gift of the Broome collection of two thousand plants from North America and elsewhere. The collection, transferred from C.E. Broome's garden at Batheaston in 1887, marked the beginning of the Botanic Gardens as we know them today. Plants were donated by others, too: Lady Lushington gave the whole of her valuable collection of choice plants from her garden at Great Bedwyn, Wiltshire, and J.W. Morris, the first curator of the collection, donated many hardy plants, including some pines raised from Himalayan seed sent by a Mr Bagshawe. These are still thought to be growing in the Pinetum.

Canon Ellacombe also gave plants. He grew every plant he could lay his hands on, exotic and native, carefully trying out different habitats for each. As well as travelling and collecting himself, he belonged to an international network of plantsmen and botanists, and was party to a great many swopping arrangements. Between 1871 and 1876, for example, he received consignments of plants from the botanic gardens at Kew, Edinburgh, Glasnevin, Oxford, Hull, Liverpool, Glasgow, Paris, Angers, Rouen, Tours, Brussels, Berlin and Hamburg, and reciprocated to as many. Canon Ellacombe lived to a great age and is remembered for his hospitality and generosity in plant gifts. Little now survives of his former garden at Bitton Old Vicarage, which is privately owned and not open to the public.

However, two gardens established by his younger colleague, Hiatt Baker, can be viewed as part of the National Gardens Scheme. Hiatt Baker's first garden was at his parents' house, The Holmes, in Stoke Park Road, Bristol, now in the care of Bristol University. Here, from 1872, he developed a naturalistic garden, with a rockery with linked pools where he grew a wide range of alpines and unusual aquatic plants. But it is for the garden at Oaklands (Plate 28) in Almondsbury that he is best known. Here he established an extensive collection of trees and shrubs, and built a pond, a rockery, and a Japanese garden (though not all the plants he used were Japanese). To grace the garden, he imported large pieces of Japanese garden furniture, including stone lanterns and a bridge (Fig. 55). Following the taste for Japanese art and culture, popular at the beginning of the twentieth century, Hiatt Baker also established an outstanding collection of Japanese prints – now in the Bristol Art Gallery collection. The pools in the Japanese garden have been

Fig. 55. The craze for Japanese gardens – stone lantern at Oaklands.

partially restored by the Avon Gardens Trust.

Hiatt Baker's interest in collecting and growing as wide a variety of plants as possible has been continued by his daughter and son-in-law, Professor and Mrs Hewer; accounts of their botanical expeditions to Iran and Afghanistan in 1969 and 1971 can be found in the *Journal of the Royal Horticultural Society* (Vols XCVI, 1971 and XCVIII, 1973). At Vine House in Henbury the Hewers have created an exquisite garden which includes cuttings from many of the plants at Oaklands, as well as plants discovered on expedition.

Nurseries

In response to increased demand for forest trees and ornamental exotics, nurseries boomed in the nineteenth century. Aided by improved communications, especially the railway, new nurseries sprang up all over the country, where previously they had been concentrated in London. Matthew's *Directory of Bristol* lists seven nurserymen in 1821, and fifteen in 1870. In the account books of the Tortworth estate there are records of payments in 1850 on several different occasions 'To Charfield Station, Carriage of Plants from London'.

The firm of Sweet and Miller went bankrupt in 1837, but was taken over by James Garaway who had worked for the firm for some ten years. A bill of 1827 gives some idea of the quantities of stock held. The business of introducing new plants was clearly fraught with difficulties, for William Maule's nursery in Stapleton, which specialised in conifers, American bog plants and orchids, also went bankrupt. In 1895, Canon Ellacombe, writing about *Pyrus maulei* (now *Chaenomeles japonica*) noted that it:

> has almost a sad history. It was introduced from Japan about twenty years
> ago by Mr Maule, who was so struck with the abundance of the golden
> little quinces, that he gave up many acres in its cultivation; but the results
> to him were in every way disastrous and even hastened his death.

In Bath, the mature trees of the suburban gardens in Weston are a reminder of the stocks of the Victoria Nursery, run by Salter and Scammell and later by Salter and Wheeler, next to Royal Victoria Park. In the first edition of *The Gardeners' Chronicle*, in 1840, they were advertising a new ipomoea (morning glory). In 1847, Edward Titley, also of Bath, 'offered to the world' his new fuchsia, 'Jenny Lind'.

Nineteenth-century maps of both Bristol and Bath show extensive areas given over to nurseries, and the Whitehall, Stapleton, Frenchay and Kingswood areas were noted for their market gardens.

Public Parks and Gardens

Until the middle of the nineteenth century, pleasure gardens, with some notable exceptions, were the domain of the wealthy. For the poor, there was little time for leisure, and in any event most work took place in the open air. However, the spectacular growth of population which accompanied the Industrial Revolution was concentrated in the towns, and the new working class of landless labourers found themselves crammed into overcrowded warrens of back-to-back housing without the benefit of open space. These industrial towns of the nineteenth century were a new phenomenon, a form of social organisation that grew at an uncontrollable pace, their character determined by the needs of industry. Cheap, shoddy housing huddled among factories and waste-tips; lack of sanitation and wage-slavery manifested themselves in disease and unrest. The 1840s epidemics of cholera prompted the beginnings of the Public Health Movement, and a gradual recognition of the benefits of fresh air and pleasant surroundings.

Bristol

In Bristol it was, though, a slow process. It took forty years for changes in attitude to result in the laying out of public parks in the poorer parts of town. By this time the more enlightened private landowners, including the Beauforts at Stoke Park and the Smyths at Ashton Court, were already encouraging local people to use their grounds for certain acceptable pastimes: for cricket, fishing, walking and listening to concerts.

In Bristol, the tradition of publicly owned land went back a long way, to soon after the Conquest. Brandon Hill had, with the exception of 4 acres/1.6 hectares at its summit, been granted to the Corporation by Robert Fitzharding, Earl of Gloucester (of Bristol Castle) in 1174. He made a gift of the summit to the Abbey of Tewkesbury, which built a tiny chapel there, dedicated to St Brendan, patron saint of seafarers. The chapel fell into disuse after the Reformation, and the land was bought from the Crown by Bristol Corporation in 1581 for £30. Public access to the hill is maintained, and the traditional right to dry clothes and beat out rugs there is still proclaimed in bylaws displayed on notices in the park. Cabot Tower was erected on the summit in 1897 to commemorate the four hundredth anniversary of the explorer's Atlantic voyage (Fig. 56), and the rock and water garden below the tower was completed in 1936 by the City, which has recently announced plans to restore the area. In the last few years The Wildlife Trust has managed some of the grassland, with the aim of increasing the number of species of wildflowers.

College Green, flanked by the Cathedral and the Council House, was originally the green of the manor of Billeswick, also owned by Robert Fitzharding. In 1140 it became St Augustine's Green, the burial ground of the Abbey of Tewkesbury, and although as the Port of Bristol grew the Abbey lands were swallowed up, the Green remained, enclosed by railings and graced with avenues of trees, but open to the public. Now owned by the Dean and Chapter of Bristol Cathedral, it has been leased to the City of Bristol since 1894. When the Green was lowered in 1950, in homage to the Council House, it lost its mature trees and much of its character. Today, although the recent road closure has restored some of its tranquillity, the landscaping lacks the robust character of the Victorian layout.

The earliest provision of public space was in the wealthier areas of the city – Queen Square and St James's Square were, as we have seen, developed early in the

Fig. 56. Postcard view of Cabot Tower, Bristol, c.1915.

eighteenth century. In 1861, the use of Clifton and Durdham Downs was secured in perpetuity for the people of Bristol by Act of Parliament, but provision close to the burgeoning industrial areas was yet to come; the first public parks were still twenty years away. Despite major changes in the material fabric of society, the social structure had altered little. The paternalism inherent in the English class system reappeared with renewed force in the second half of the nineteenth century. Public libraries, museums, baths, art galleries and parks could not have been built on the scale they were without the generosity of public benefactors. In Bristol, the Wills family, like the Smyths of Ashton Court, and others, were prominent in civic development.

Yet despite the beneficence of leading citizens, the provision of public parks was slow to gather momentum. An anonymous pamphlet of 1871, decades after parks had been laid out in similar industrial towns, was entitled 'A cry from the poor; a letter from sixteen working men to the sixteen aldermen of the city'. It demanded 'people's parks' in working-class areas. But land values at the time were still buoyant and nothing was done. However, the agricultural exploitation of the American prairies and improvements in trans-Atlantic transport heralded a major agricultural depression in Britain in the 1880s, which was to endure until World War I. Agricultural rents collapsed and estates began selling land which could not be economically let.

In 1883, twelve years after the pamphlet appeared, Sir Greville Smyth of Ashton Court gave to the city a piece of land in Bedminster. First called the 'People's Park',

Fig. 57. Victoria Square, Clifton, an engraving of c.1855 – communal gardens as paradise laid out in the fashionable 'gardenesque' style.

it was renamed in honour of its benefactor when he died in 1902. The Smyth estate also sold land for Perrett Park in Knowle in 1900, for Victoria Park in Bedminster in 1888, and for Eastville Park in 1884 (Plate 29).

The idea of 'parks for the people' also involved a large measure of social control. Reformers believed that the working classes could be rescued from their base recreations and morally uplifted by the passive amusement that parks could offer. Towards the end of the nineteenth century, the City took advantage of low land prices and an increase in revenue from rates to create or adopt many parks, including St George's Park (1897), St Andrew's Park (1890), St Matthias Park (1884), Canford Park (Clifton Urban Sanitary Society 1874, adopted 1902), Gaunts Ham Park (1888), Fishponds Park (1887), Sparke Evans Park (1902), St Agnes Gardens (1884) and Mina Road Park (1884). There was still no provision in the very poorest parts of the City, around Broadmead, the Dings and St Philips Marsh.

Structurally, these municipal parks were pretty much as we find them today: a mixture of informal and formal styles, often embellished with cast-iron urinals, drinking fountains, bandstands and ponds. Bowling greens were added early, fitting in with such gentle and relaxing pastimes as promenading, listening to the band or simply watching the world go by. The approved, middle-class concept of leisure proscribed physical exertion and unseemly breaking into a sweat.

Weston and Clevedon – seaside resorts

The new financial freedom that allowed the middle classes to travel on the railway, also created the seaside resort, and there the same polite tradition of leisure informed the laying out of strand parades, beach gardens and winter gardens.

Weston-super-Mare and Clevedon grew rapidly as popular resorts in the nineteenth century (Weston's population was only 163 in 1810). Private speculation and patronage fuelled much of the development so that the first generation of parks were those associated with private housing schemes; in Weston, for example, The Shrubbery, Eastfield Park and Ellenborough Park. Henry Davies was a prominent Weston builder whose work at Weston's Royal Crescent echoed the communal garden designs of Bath and Clifton. The gift of 16 acres/6.5 hectares of land by Davies's widow in 1888 enabled the creation of Clarence Park.

Fig. 58. The great tradition of pictorial carpet-bedding fully deployed in the Floral Clock at Weston-super-Mare. A postcard of 1935.

As elsewhere in the country, Weston also acquired several areas of land as public open space. Flagstaff Hill became Prince Consort Gardens, and Beach Lawns was laid out in 1885, after the construction of a new sea wall, to become the centrepiece of the promenade. The gardens of the former manor became Grove Park in 1891, and Ashcombe Park was opened to the public at the end of the nineteenth century. The Winter Gardens, planned in the 1880s were not opened until 1927 (Plate 30).

In Clevedon, Sir Arthur Halham Elton, lord of the manor of Clevedon, was the town's principal benefactor. He gave the town its libraries, cottage hospital, many of its streets and villas, and several public parks. Alexandra Gardens, Herbert Gardens and Pier Copse were gifts from Elton in the 1860s. The two late nineteenth-century parks of Green Beach and Walton Gardens were laid out by the Council, while Sunhill Park (Clevedon Community Centre) began life as the garden to an early twentieth-century house. In Portishead, the Lake Ground, dominated by the Marine Lake, was established in 1910.

Bath

The City of Bath prospered and grew as a Georgian playground and spa. Many of its eighteenth-century gardens, parks and walks were integral to the design of its elegant terraces and squares. Others were created by public subscription or run on a commercial basis, like Sydney Gardens (1795) which was only taken over by the Council after World War I.

Royal Victoria Park, the second public park in the country after Regent's Park, was established by private subscription in 1820 on land donated by the Freemen of Bath, and opened to the public by Princess Victoria in 1830. Designed by the City architect, it was developed and maintained by a committee of wealthy citizens until the Council took it over in 1921 (Fig. 59). By then the Victoria Column (an obelisk), bandstand and various urns, statues and ornamental gateways had been added.

As well as being an important amenity, Victoria Park also became known for its plants, which equalled the fine collection of the Derby arboretum. The collection was meticulously labelled, and included the latest discoveries. The Wellingtonia (*Sequoiadendron giganteum*), for example, was introduced to England in 1853 (by Messrs Veitch) and was already present in Victoria Park in 1855. And subscribers, who underwrote the park financially until 1923, also made vital donations of plants; in 1844 the committee's report included a list of desiderata. From 1830 to 1855 a horticultural exhibition was held each year.

The Botanic Garden (Plate 32) in a corner of the park was begun in 1840 but did not become established with any conviction until it was redesigned and extended under the direction of J.W. Morris of Kew, who made it ready to receive the C.E. Broome plant collection in 1887. The summerhouse was first shown by Bath Corporation at the British Empire Collection held at Wembley in 1924, before being erected in Victoria Park. Royal Victoria Park remains a source of civic pride and a major attraction to tourists and residents (Plate 31).

Hedgemead Park came about as the result of poorly planned speculative development. Two hundred and seventy-one houses were built on the area below Camden Crescent on unstable shale and clay substrate. The inherent instability of the geology was exacerbated by poor provision for natural drainage. The result was a series of landslips, the worst destroying one hundred and thirty-five houses in 1881. The site was subsequently acquired by the City Council and laid out as a public park in several sections, divided by the slope, rockeries and planting, the whole kept in place by a massive stone retaining wall with a turret and battlements. Henrietta Park, Bathwick, was opened in 1887.

The topography of Bath lends itself well to the creation of panoramic views,

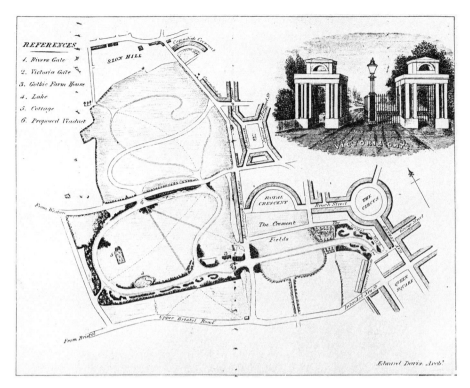

Fig. 59. Plan of Royal Victoria Park, Bath, c.1831.

which were exploited to the full at Alexandra Park and Magdalen Gardens, laid out by the City Council around the turn of the century at the top of Beechen Cliff.

Changing attitudes

Gradually, through the twentieth century, the rules against physical activity in public places were relaxed; children's playgrounds, tennis courts and sports pitches were introduced, reflecting a change from passive to active recreation. The relative bleakness of football pitches and the sad loss of ornamental ironwork, particularly railings, since World War II, have diminished the sense of safe enclosure and intimacy of design. The golden era of horticultural excellence, with a few worthy exceptions, has passed. Gone with it are the elaborate bedding schemes, the floral stairs, carpets and clocks, the nursery and glasshouse in every park (Fig. 60).

Gone, today, too, is the sense of civic pride. Changed attitudes concerning the purpose of public parks, chronic cash starvation and compulsory competitive tendering have led to an acceptance of minimal maintenance. Local authorities have all too often capitulated in the face of difficulties, too readily blamed vandalism for their abandonment of standards of excellence. The turfed flower beds, the derelict and boarded-up buildings, the dogs' mess and the litter are powerful symbols of neglect – invitations in turn to further abuse. The original

Fig. 60. The end of the line for floral displays? Paddington Bear at Bath Spa station, 1985.

purpose of public parks was to provide peaceful and beautiful refuge from the pressures and congestion of city life, where the city dweller could retreat to enjoy fresh air, to mingle or to contemplate, to reconnect with nature. The distance between those ideals and present management present a greater threat to the future of our parks than they have ever faced before.

Institution Gardens

Many of our large institutions – hospitals, schools, workhouses and reformatories – originated in the Victorian era. Their grounds have often remained relatively unchanged, some in fact preserving landscapes from periods before the institution itself came into being, so that they have become increasingly important contributors to the quality of the local environment. But policy changes and increased government pressure on administrative authorities, together with increased pressure for building land, have made the future of institution gardens in Avon particularly uncertain. The sale of school playing fields for housing has become all too familiar, but it is the health authorities in particular which have been under pressure to dispose of their large and historic landholdings.

Provision for the welfare of the poor, the nursing of the sick, and the education of children has always been a social concern; prior to industrialisation on a large scale, it was chiefly the Church, the paternalism of the aristocracy, or charitable bodies which met these needs. But relief under the old Poor Law was inadequate to cope with the conditions of the Industrial Revolution; the new Poor Law of 1832 introduced a punitive attitude towards those unable to work; and Victorian *laissez-faire* economics justified the workhouse, the poorhouse and the mental institution.

However, a more enlightened attitude towards the poor gradually emerged towards the end of the nineteenth century in the wake of the Public Health Movement. Legislation for the care of the mentally handicapped and the mentally ill coincided with the demise of the great estates from the 1880s. Country seats and parkland became available at knock-down prices as the aristocracy and squirearchy adjusted to leaner times. The Reverend Harold Burden's 'Colony' system of national institutions for the mentally handicapped, for example, were established from 1908 in a string of country houses purchased after they failed to reach their reserve prices at auction.

Brislington House – and 'muscular exertions'

Private sector care for the wealthy insane had appeared much earlier. Dr Edward Long Fox pioneered humane treatment with the establishment of Brislington House in 1804, the first private asylum built in this country. The main building was designed as a grand mansion and the grounds were laid out in picturesque style, ornamented with woods and cottages. The 200 acres/80 hectares of park and gardens were central to Fox's enlightened beliefs in patient care, and the kitchen gardens and model farm allowed self-sufficiency in food. A prospectus of 1836 illustrates Dr Fox's radical prescriptions and the uses to which the land was put.

Fig. 61. Swiss cottage in the grounds of Brislington House. Such elegant houses were built for the privacy of more affluent patients. Painting by T.L.S. Rowbotham, 1827.

Located next to the main Bristol to Bath road, it was an area 'where the proprietor could not be incommoded by neighbours', which was 'laid out in diversified walks and extensive plantations that afford shelter and security from all intrusion'. Fox's treatment depended on 'moral and physical management' in 'perfect security' while maintaining 'a great degree of liberty'. 'Constant access to the open air' and 'muscular exertions' were considered 'the most favourable employment for the insane'. Fox had separate cottages constructed around the perimeter of the site for the patient requiring to be kept 'at some little distance from scenes that may engage too much of his attention'. In practice, it appears that these cottages were occupied by wealthy patients, who were 'allowed to pursue any style of living and expense as to carriages, horses etc . . . most suitable to their former habits' (Fig. 61). The venture was a commercial success, and a copy of the Brislington layout was established in open country at Northwoods in Winterbourne Parish in 1832.

The Stapleton Workhouse
The outlook for the poor was considerably bleaker. In 1833, the Bristol Corporation of the Poor took over the old 'French Prison' in Stapleton as a workhouse. The hardship and misery of life in Stapleton Workhouse (later Manor Park Hospital, now Blackberry Hill Hospital) have been documented by local historians. Here there was no garden at all. 'In a bleak and isolated place, dominated by its high stone walls, the grey and forbidding exterior loomed over the neighbourhood.'

The Bristol Mental Hospital (Glenside)
The Bristol Mental Hospital, now Glenside, was built on land adjacent to the Stapleton Workhouse in 1861, the Corporation making a fine job of the buildings, described by Tim Mowl (*Last Age of the Merchant Princes*, 1991) as 'like a West Country San Gimignano or the palace of some inland Doge'. Around the hospital were extensive grounds which included Reptonesque riverside woodland walks as well as ornamental planting, ponds and aviaries. From the annual reports of 1862 we learn that 'rustic summerhouses were erected in the front gardens'. In 1870, 'an avenue of limes has been planted along the front of the Asylum'. Sporadic improvements to the grounds continued. In 1887, 'a boundary walk is being made around the estate', and a bowling green was added ten years later. Bedding-out became more popular. In 1906, '4000 plants were sent in by the gardener'.

Brentry Hill
Alcoholism was another spectre haunting the moral landscape of Victorian England. The Reverend and Mrs Burden, who had worked for the homeless in London's East End with Octavia Hill, set up the country's first Inebriate Reformatory at Brentry Hill in Bristol in 1898. The villa and landscape here had been built by Humphry and John Adey Repton in 1802. Two villages were constructed in the 92 acres/37 hectares of park – one for men and one for women

Plate 32. Bath Botanic Garden has an excellent collection of trees and shrubs – and its cunning design makes it a place that is full of atmosphere.

Plate 33. The great cemetery at Arno's Vale in Bristol, a flamboyant Victorian necropolis, is a marvellous piece of nineteenth-century romantic landscaping.

Plate 34. New parterres at Badminton House, with wonderful old parkland beyond.

Plate 35. Oakwood, Bath, in May 1991, after the great storm.

Plate 36. A sparkling cascade at Widcombe Manor, on the edge of Bath.

*Plate 37 (right). Blaise Castle –
'embosom'd high' – a lovely
backdrop to public space.
Plate 38 (below). The
Palladian bridge at Prior Park.*

Plate 39. The Beaufort Memorial in its sylvan setting at Stoke Park.

Plate 40. The site of the early Tudor knot garden at Thornbury Castle.

Plate 41. The future of the past? Development threatens to engulf the surroundings of the Black Castle at Arno's Court.

– with the declared aim that 'as far as possible, the ordinary life of an English village prevails – without the drink'; and presumably without the courting.

Again we find the familiar principles of fresh air and exercise, although this time an existing landscape was adapted to the needs of the institution. The domesticated landscape of an English country park was eminently suited to its new role. The villa became an administration centre; hothouses, kitchen gardens and flower beds provided work for the inmates; and there were woodland walks and fields for recreation. The temptations of the city were suitably distant.

Brentry remained in institutional use until the National Health Service took it over, and proposals to build on the land to the south were rejected by the Department of the Environment in 1990. Despite the land's now utilitarian appearance, the Department accepted the Avon Gardens Trust's case that it was part of the parkland setting of the listed house, and that it had historic landscape value in its own right.

Stoke Park and the 'Colony' system
In 1908 Burden leased Stoke Park from the 10th Duke of Beaufort as the nucleus of the first national institution for the mentally handicapped in the country. The 'Colony' system was later able to exploit funds available under the Mental Health Act of 1911, and also use the captive labour of the inmates. Not only self-sufficient in food, it also produced boots and shoes, furniture and tools, and carried out its own laundry and maintenance. Quickly outgrowing Stoke Park, the Colony expanded before World War I into a string of historic country houses in the area: at Leigh Court, Heath House, Stapleton Grove and Hanham Hall.

Stoke Park Hospital, Bristol.

Fig. 62. Aerial view of Stoke Park Hospital. Postcard of c.1950.

Fig. 63. Arcadian landscape becomes high security compound. Leigh Court today – a case study of planning failure.

It was due to Burden's acquisition of country estates that Frenchay Health Authority inherited a large and important legacy of designed landscapes. Under pressure to sell them for maximum capital gain, the health authority has found itself in conflict with amenity groups and planning authorities over redevelopment proposals, with various consequences for the historic grounds. Stoke Park is largely derelict; a housing scheme has recently been approved at Stapleton Grove (Purdown Hospital); at Heath House a private institution has promised to restore the landscape; a proposal for fifty houses at Brentry was defeated at appeal; and Leigh Court has been split into several ownerships and parts of the Repton landscape have been destroyed. Most of the woods at Leigh Court (Fig. 63) had already been acquired by the Forestry Commission, but the complete break-up of the estate has resulted in serious damage to its historic character, with fencing and hedging across the parkland, car-parking for a failed business centre, and hideous agricultural development involving a vast amount of spoil-tipping in the once Arcadian valley below Abbot's Leigh village. It has been remarked that every county should have a Leigh Court to show just what can go wrong with a historic landscape (Fig.63). Nevertheless, the Freeways Trust, which occupies the old home farm buildings, has done sterling work on restoring the woodlands, and the new owners of the house have commisssioned a restoration plan for their part of the estate.

Educational establishments

Two notable Bristol schools – Clifton College (1862) and Bristol Grammar School (1879) – were built during the High Victorian period, their layout and design reflecting the style of the country house. Both are grand Gothic piles with formal landscaping – terraces and avenues near the buildings, and specimen planting in the grounds.

Colston School was established at Bishop Monk's park in Stapleton in 1861, and evidence of an ambitious picturesque layout can still be found in the riverside walks which lead through rock tunnels and over outcrops, in particular the Black Rocks, a well-known beauty spot. The architect John Norton's design for St Matthias College (1852) in Fishponds was a masterpiece of toy-town Gothic; the buildings being enhanced by a sunken lawn, a knot garden, and a collection of unusual trees including an exceptionally large Judas tree.

Other institutions – and the future?

Two estates straddling the A38 Bristol to Gloucester road at Falfield were also put to institutional use. Eastwood Park, Lord Liverpool's 1840s landscape park on a medieval deer park, was commandeered as a Civil Defence training establishment during the last war. It became a National Health Service training centre, and was recently declared surplus to requirements. Proposals for massive housing development, dismissed by the Secretary of State, were followed by a scheme for a theme park. Currently, the Department of Health aspires to restructure the site, build some new houses, and hand part of the park to the local authority for public use. However, the future of this beautiful historic site remains uncertain.

Tortworth Park was put to military use. The Royal Navy used the lake to test amphibious vehicles in preparation for the D-Day landings. After the war, the house was converted for use by the Prison Service, which still maintains the arboretum, and the formal gardens were grubbed up and replaced by lawns. The house was later sold to a private buyer who intended to put it to philanthropic use for the care of vagrant men, but this great Victorian house was partially gutted by fire during restoration. Work was brought to a halt, which has allowed decay and dereliction a free hand. So the wheel turns.

Most of the historic landscapes described above could be lost within the next decade. They deserve to survive for their contribution to the environment, to the evolution of landscape design in the county, and for the richness of their human history.

Cemeteries

The Garden Cemetery Movement in the early part of the century came about as a reaction to insanitary and multiple burials, to pollution of drinking water supplies, and to body snatching and disturbance of graves.

Existing churchyards were unable to cope with the overwhelming mortality rates in the newly crowded urban areas. Bodies were being buried and then disinterred to make room for new burials, with indecent haste. Added to the outcries of the sanitary reformers were the demands of the dissenting religions for non-denominational burial in consecrated ground.

Churchyard burial was banned in Paris in 1804, and the first garden cemetery laid out to the east of the city in open countryside. The Cemetery of Père-Lachaise features formal avenues, winding paths and trees. It became the model for nineteenth-century cemetery design. In England, cemeteries laid out in the style of the informal landscape park predated municipal parks as public open spaces by thirty years.

John Claudius Loudon had enormous influence on English cemetery design, by combining sanitary and landscape design theory and promoting the efforts of people like John Strang, mastermind of the Glasgow Necropolis of 1831. On its hillside site, the Necropolis displayed an amazing collection of memorials of every conceivable architectural type – Classical, Gothic, Moorish and Oriental – producing the effect of a City of the Dead raised in splendour above the town. Loudon described its effect, which delighted him, as 'grand and melancholy'. Loudon wrote on every aspect of cemetery design, overlooking none of the details. He recommended individual interment in wooden coffins in graves 6 feet/1.8 metres deep, with the whole site bounded and protected by high walls and gates, and the added security of lodges or watch-houses to guard against the activities of the 'Resurrection Men', the body snatchers who supplied surgeons with fresh cadavers for dissection.

Loudon and the Garden Cemetery Movement banished the horrible spectre of bone-strewn, flooded or desecrated graveyards, and mouldy or slimy vaults, and replaced them with Arcadian landscapes, gardens designed to be health-giving and evocative of 'contemplative creation'. Loudon also saw the potential of cemeteries for educational use:

> a general cemetery in the neighbourhood of a town, properly designed, laid out, ornamented with tombs, planted with trees, shrubs, and herbacous plants, all named, and the whole properly kept, might become a school of instruction in architecture, sculpture, landscape gardening, arboriculture, botany, and in those important parts of general gardening, neatness, order, and high keeping.

The success of Loudon's theories may be judged today in his design for Abbey Cemetery in Ralph Allen Drive in Bath. This was laid out in the early 1840s on a steeply sloping site that took advantage of wide views over Bath which James Tunstall described in his *Rambles about Bath and its Neighbourhood*:

> From the Cemetery we obtain varied and extensive views of the most beautiful description. The bank of Beechen Cliff forms a noble prospect, towering 360 feet [108 metres] above the city, which with its churches, the Abbey rising in the midst, stretches up the height of Lansdown. Below to the westward is Bagatelle, formerly a public tea garden, and Perrymead, with the road leading through the romantically situated archway to Pope's favourite walk; eastward the picturesque ivy covered tower of Widcombe old church, with its manor house and hanging plantation rising above its rural graveyard; to the south, the grounds of Prior Park; while Lyncome

Hill, with its diversified scenery, contributes to the calm enjoyment of those who walk in sadness among the graves of the beloved dead . . .

The mortuary chapel, designed by Bath architect G.P. Manners in the Norman style, was prominently placed at the head of the cemetery.

Arno's Vale

Bristol's best-known cemetery is at Arno's Vale (Plate 33), distinguished as the only cemetery in the County of Avon to be included on the English Heritage Register of Parks and Gardens of Special Historic Interest. The degree of Loudon's influence is unknown, but the layout conforms to his recipe for good design. Although overgrown and neglected in places, the grandeur of this 1837 design is still evident.

A pair of neo-Classical lodges with porticos on fluted Doric columns flank the entrance gates. Curving processional routes, decorated with imposing monuments, give way to serpentine paths which wend between hillside plots. The Church of England Chapel, a small yet monumental building with giant Corinthian pilasters, contrasts with the unadorned Dissenters' Chapel. Both chapels, the lodges and the entrance gates are by Charles Underwood, *c*.1840 and all are grade II* listed buildings. There is a twentieth-century war memorial in the style of a five-bay arched loggia, grand and austere, and an exotic fancy of a tomb in the Indian Romantic manner. This commemorates Rajah Rammohun Roy Bahador, the great Hindu religious reformer and humanist, who died on a visit to Stapleton Grove. Originally buried there, his remains were removed to this most splendid of tombs erected by his followers and admirers in 1843.

Greenbank

Abbey Cemetery and Arno's Vale Cemetery are the quintessence of garden cemetery design in the county, but there are others, less dramatic perhaps, in all urban localities in Avon. Greenbank in Bristol, opened in 1871, is a good example of an Arcadian layout, with its avenue of limes and winding walks, and a symmetrical pair of Gothic chapels as the central focus of the landscape, functioning visually in the same manner as an eighteenth-century country house. Cemeteries, unlike public parks and town squares, were exempt from the removal of railings during World War II; the stout ornate gates and railings at Greenbank show how important they must have been to the character of municipal parks. The chapels at Greenbank are now redundant, but plans by Bristol City Council to demolish them met with fierce opposition from the local community, the Victorian Society and the Avon Gardens Trust; they are now listed as buildings of architectural or historic interest. However, for want of a new use, they are rapidly becoming derelict.

Garden cemeteries, as well as being sacred memorials to loved ones and ancestors, continue to provide welcome relief from urban congestion, especially in areas, like Greenbank, where they are the only open space. They also provide a fascinating design link between the informal landscape park of the eighteenth century and the formalised municipal parks of the late nineteenth century.

Chapter 6

After the Great War

AS A RESULT of major social and economic changes, landscape gardening and garden design in Britain suffered a long decline after World War I. Agricultural depression, death duties, scarce and expensive labour and, surprisingly often, the withering of male lineage, have all played a part in the downfall of the country house, its gardens and its landscape park. Many estates sold their farms, leaving only a core landscape without income from agricultural rents to fund its maintenance. Others, like Cleve Hill at Downend, were broken up and built over with housing estates. Some became public parks while others were pressed into institutional use – schools, colleges, and hospitals all taking advantage of cheap and extensive sites.

Although new uses counteracted the redundancy of many parks, thereby protecting them from wholesale redevelopment, they have almost always damaged the detail and sometimes the structure of the layouts. Piecemeal development, and management which placed little value on the historic landscape, have generally been made worse by a lack of awareness of the site's history, a lack of recognition of its importance, and insufficient resources for its upkeep. Until recently, too, public interest in this part of our heritage has been limited, with a consequent lack of support.

The results of the problems faced by parks and gardens can be seen at many of the county's most historically important sites. The gardens at Stoke Park have been built over, the lake filled in for the M32, the house and landscape left derelict. Capability Brown's design at Newton Park has lost most of its planting, and a muddle of buildings crowd the mansion. Kelston Park languishes under a scrubby blanket, the park growing arable weeds in set-aside, the woods and lodge in ruins. Kingsweston is hardly recognisable as a park at all; while the parkland at Leigh Court has been chopped into paddocks, subdivided by post and wire fences and

Fig. 64. The castellated entrance to Beckford's Ride.

unsympathetic planting. Repton's design at Brentry is now largely barren, and his three parks in the ownership of Bristol City Council – Ashton Court, Blaise Castle and Oldbury Court – have all suffered from uncertain management and financial stringency. The same is true of municipal parks, historic designs in their own right, where features have gradually disappeared and maintenance has been trimmed to the bone. The romantic dishevelment of Arno's Vale Cemetery has tipped towards dereliction, and Beckford's Ride is no longer true to its name, its course fragmented by a dozen different ownerships (Fig. 64).

A shortage of labour and its higher price in the wake of the war meant that labour-intensive work was the first to go. The walled kitchen gardens of country houses became redundant, their glasshouses and frames collapsing. Flower beds were grassed over and the ubiquitous lawn became the internationally recognised characteristic of British gardening, owing its popularity to improved mowing technology. Flowering shrubs have replaced labour-intensive herbaceous borders and rose gardens. The Victorian massed bedding schemes of half-hardy annuals and tropical plants have disappeared in all but the best kept municipal parks and seaside gardens.

Victorian rock gardens for displaying alpines are also under threat. Once abandoned, the plants are rapidly enveloped in perennial weeds which are almost impossible to eradicate. The once famous rock garden of Sir Stanley White at Hollywood Tower in Northavon was plundered in 1966 by the present owners, Bristol Zoo, to extend their own gardens in Clifton. The condition of what remains is not known. Specialist interest in rock plants and gardens continues in Avon, but on a much smaller scale and mostly in private gardens, like the impressive collection at Severn View near Thornbury. In public sites their care has generally been abandoned, though the remains of earlier rockeries can still be found in some parks. In Fishponds Park, for instance, discarded but still handsome rockwork peeks out from the deep shade of an evergreen bush. However, the extensive rock garden at Brandon Hill, around the foot of Cabot Tower, is due to be revitalised by Bristol City Council.

Perhaps one of the most threatened types of garden is that of substantial town and suburban houses. Only a few are of special importance as gardens, but many more are important to the townscape and as an integral part of historic town plans. The greatest enemy of these gardens is tarmac. As land values rise steeply in historic towns and cities, these gardens are sold for commercial or public use, turned over to car parking or built over as suitable 'infill' sites. Two of the saddest losses recently were of Stanley Badock's turn-of-the-century gardens at Holmwood and Southmead Manor. Planning permission for infill housing was granted at the former, despite its being in a conservation area, and the latter was bulldozed by an impatient developer who could not get planning permission.

The movement for the conservation and restoration of historic parks and gardens has identified and attempted to address these problems, so that the best of our landscape heritage might be re-evaluated and revitalised. The whole point of parks and gardens is that they were laid out for pleasure and enjoyment: they are the culmination of an art form which obsessed English society for two hundred years, and which are recognised as our greatest contribution to European art. There are signs, at last, that the tide may be turning in their favour. This chapter describes some of the recent developments in Avon's garden history and what has been done in the field of conservation.

Gardening in the Twentieth Century

The Dower House and Badminton House

Recent developments in English gardening have been limited in scale and scope, and have tended to remain nostalgic in spirit. In the previous chapter we saw how, around the turn of the century, leading gardeners began to combine wild gardening and formal gardening – the two principal styles of the nineteenth century. The pioneer of this synthesis, Gertrude Jekyll, inspired the work of Russell Page, who collaborated with the Duchess of Beaufort on two local gardens: the Dower House (The Cottage) in Badminton village, and more recently, Badminton House itself. The garden at the Dower House, laid out between 1964 and 1984, is a perfect example of formal enclosures bounded by neat hedges and climber-covered walls in the Hidcote manner, containing complex and subtle colour schemes in the Jekyll tradition.

The garden is big by modern standards but appears even more so because of the imaginative succession of spaces linked by intriguing vistas. The main axis from the house leads up steps flanked by clipped yew pyramids to a square plot bordered by mixed plantings of soft blue, purple, pink and pale yellow with silver foliage. Concealed behind an ancient yew hedge is a swimming pool, a twentieth-century feature which could be difficult to assimilate, but is designed here with great simplicity and restraint to become a feature in the garden plan. Among the many intimate enclosures are a pond garden with yew hedges around a circular central fountain pool, enclosing densely planted corners with narrow paths and box hedges, and a walled kitchen garden with its neat rows of vegetables and soft fruits.

Russell Page's garden on the east front of Badminton House, his last design before he died, was again defined by box parterres and yew hedges. The new garden on the south front is by the Belgian designer François Goffinet (Plate 34). This is in four sections. Adjoining the kitchen is a herb garden, next to which are two pools, then a grass oval and a silver and white border all edged in hornbeam (*Carpinus betulus*). At the bottom of the garden are old-fashioned roses in box-edged beds, while a further section of the garden uses plants for seasonal display.

Essex House

Between 1961 and 1971 Alvilde Lees-Milne created a garden at Alderley Grange in Gloucestershire, notable for an especially fine herb garden. Since 1975 she has created a new garden at Essex House in Badminton village – an excellent example of what can be achieved in the small gardens of the twentieth century by the use of enclosure and changes in level, giving a sense of space, and by the use of carefully chosen colour schemes in the planting.

Lyegrove House

The grounds of Lyegrove House, near Badminton, first laid out in the seventeenth century, now have a good example of twentieth-century gardening resulting from a collaboration between architect and artist plantswoman. The architect G.H. Kitchin was employed in 1927 to design the walled garden, gateways, gazebos and pools, while the planting was chosen and developed by the owner, the Countess of Westmoreland.

Hill House

The garden laid out from 1968 by Sally, Duchess of Westminster at Hill House in Wickwar exhibits a clever blending of colours in its borders, together with labour-saving ground-cover planting. Here a striking sweep of lawn is fringed with shrubby borders that advance and recede like stage wings to create a series of interesting spaces. The planting is rich and mixed with frequent use of plants for foliage effect, especially silver and gold, and there is a marvellous collection of old roses.

Vine House and Orchard House

Interest has continued into the latter half of the twentieth century in the creation of specialised plant habitats. The garden at Vine House in Henbury contains a number of these within an area of only 2 acres/0.8 hectares, and is a good demonstration of how a clever design can bring a diversity of planting habitats into a unified whole. Another good example is to be found at Orchard House in Claverton, a garden created by Rear-Admiral and Mrs Tracy.

Widcombe Manor and Crowe Hall

Two registered historic gardens in Bath have continued to be reshaped in the twentieth century. One is Widcombe Manor, built in 1727 with a formal garden which was completely remodelled, probably by Harold Peto, in the Italianate style. Since 1970 modern planting has been added to the garden.

The second is Crowe Hall, further up the hill from Widcombe Manor, an eighteenth-century garden reshaped in nineteenth-century 'villa' style. Since 1961, new elements have been superimposed by the Barratt family. Former fruit and vegetable gardens on the terraces below the house have been adapted successfully for an enormous variety of flowering trees and shrubs. Masses of spring bulbs have been planted among established fruit trees, and impressive displays of flowers in baskets and tubs make a striking feature.

Camerton Court

Perhaps the most ambitious reworking of an earlier layout is being shaped at Camerton Court. Only a canal and some survivors of the early nineteenth-century tree planting remained when the overgrown site was cleared in the 1980s. Since then, new layouts are being introduced, and a host of new 'historical' features have been added, including a temple, a cascade, gazebos, a formal pond with a fountain and urns, and an orangery. Major new plantings make an unusual juxtaposition with traditional garden buildings. What makes this site so interesting is the insight it provides into the design practices of the past, and the opportunity to see a grand layout in its infancy. Trees and shrubs are moved around, by trial and error, to achieve the best effect, and the development of the garden goes ahead by a mixture of design, accident and inspiration.

The 'Wild' Garden Today

The 'wild' garden, first given popular expression by William Robinson, has continued in the twentieth century with naturalistic gardens making use of a wide variety of trees and large shrubs, underplanted with bulbs and naturalising plants. Good examples are to be found in John Naish's garden at Algar's Manor, Iron Acton, John Maycock's Brackenwood Nurseries at Portishead, and Major Lock's garden at Rainbow Wood in Bath. Of particular note is Keith Steadman's garden at Westend House in Wickwar. Developed since 1950, this is a distinctive garden arranged for minimum maintenance, in which the foliage and form of the trees and shrubs, their stem colour and fruit are of more importance in the year-round effect than the more ephemeral flowers. In eighteenth-century fashion the boundaries are concealed to make the modest area (3 acres/1.2 hectares) seem larger and the winding paths provide mystery and surprise.

And Wildlife Gardening

In the 1970s and 1980s nature conservation became a major issue, and popular interest has resulted in a fashion for 'wildlife gardening'. Today no suburban garden is complete without its nesting boxes, native wildflowers, and wildlife pond. In Avon, the Wildlife Trust has taken a lead in promoting wildlife gardening at Brandon Hill and at its own site at Willsbridge Mill in Kingswood. The butterfly borders, rockeries, pond and bog garden are all dedicated to Canon Ellacombe, the great nineteenth-century plant enthusiast.

Public Parks

In the reconstruction after World War II, Bristol City Council reworked many of the city's smaller open spaces. College Green was lowered in 1950, and John Norton's 1851 copy of the High Cross was removed to Berkeley Square (the original is at Stourhead). St James's Park, on the site of Bristol's oldest churchyard, was remodelled, and the Friends' Garden for the Blind was laid out in 1954, originally with fragrant plants, on the site of the Quaker Friends Burial Ground, tucked away by Redcliffe roundabout. King Square was replanted with the ubiquitous flowering cherries of the period, and some of the city's smaller communal gardens, for example Fremantle Square with its magnificent solitary holm oak, were taken into council ownership.

Public parks never really recovered from the loss of their railings (removed to be melted down for armaments), either aesthetically or in their sense of protective enclosure. Once they could not be locked at night, abuse and vandalism became more common.

Castle Park

The overall picture of open space provision in Bristol since the war, considering the growth in population and prosperity, has been disappointing. Few new public parks, other than new playing fields, have been created, although an important exception is Castle Park on the site of Bristol Castle, which was the hub of Bristol's main shopping area until flattened by the Luftwaffe in the Blitz. Casson, Condor and Partners were commissioned in the mid 1960s to produce a plan for re-use of the area as a public park, retaining and enhancing the scant remains of the castle and the bomb-ruined St Peter's Church. The plan included a palm house, formal layouts for a herb garden, water garden and avenue of trees, and informal stretches of grass and trees and a children's play area.

Castle Park as realised omitted most of these features, but nevertheless became a popular lunchtime spot for shoppers and office workers. Now, Bristol City Council have completed the redesign of the park, making more of the archaeological remains of the Castle Keep, Newgate and the Barbican, as well as adding a new landing stage, bandstand with arena and a playground.

Country parks

The decline in popularity of the municipal park as the venue for family outings, promenading and 'walking out', together with the freedom brought by the railway and then by the motor car, has increased the demand for access to the countryside for recreation and enjoyment. This led to the setting up in the 1960s and 1970s of Country Parks – open access areas of intensively managed countryside, which, with their car parks, picnic sites and nature trails, are as much designed landscapes as the historic parklands they often incorporate.

Ashton Court, although not officially designated as a Country Park, was pressed into this role, somewhat to the detriment of its historic character. However, the City Council has prepared an extensive management plan for its long-term future, under which it will have to – and can – accommodate a wide variety of amenity uses. Chew Valley Lake, managed by the Water Authority, performs a similar function. Proposals for Hengrove Park in South Bristol, and Eastwood Park at Falfield, see them developing as major recreational attractions.

Municipal open space

However, the municipal park still offers the most familiar and accessible open space recreation to most people. Their great horticultural traditions have largely disappeared in Bristol, but fragments of the Victorian park ideal flourish in the tourist areas of Bath and at the seaside resorts, where some of the delights of colourful bedding schemes, floral clocks and anniversary designs can still be enjoyed (Fig. 60).

A number of smaller initiatives in open space management have been started, including woodland planting and management projects in the Bristol urban fringe, the creation of amenity open spaces around the Bristol City Docks, and the provision of 'pocket parks' like Owen Square in Easton to serve the needs of local people. Begbrook Community Park has recently been opened on land left to the City of Bristol by the Vassal family of Oldbury Court, under a covenant restricting its use to public open space.

These ventures aside, the story remains one of too little, too late. Earlier designs in Bristol's historic estates, such as Ashton Court, Blaise Castle and Oldbury Court, have become increasingly blurred by self-regenerated scrub woodland and ill-advised planting schemes. Beautiful and inviting layouts of woodland walks and grassy banks which survived into the 1960s and 1970s have become overgrown and smothered by bramble and scrub, and are now unattractive to the public.

Historic Parks and Gardens – down but not out

Gardening is not just an art associated with great country houses, but touches everyone and every kind of building: cottages, semi-detached and terrace houses, schools, hospitals, offices and factories, squares, crescents and public parks. Yet while the buildings can, if maintained and used, be preserved for an indefinite period, gardens need constant attention to balance the continuous cycles of growth, maturity, decay and renewal. Gardening styles go out of fashion like clothes. 'Fussy' and 'garish' Victorian bedding schemes have been condemned as vulgar and banished. But the concern with period detail that is shown in restoring, decorating and furnishing the fabric of historic (including Victorian and Edwardian) houses has only just begun to appear in historic gardens.

Public interest in visiting historic parks and gardens has grown dramatically over the last decade. In 1992, when the overall level of visitors to all attractions fell, the numbers visiting parks and gardens rose. The most popular venue nationally was Roundhay Park in Leeds, a municipal park kept to the highest order and realising its potential. The increased public interest over the last decade suggests that the restoration of sites, even of those that have been largely forgotten or ignored, is a realistic and desirable possibility. They clearly have a major role to play in outdoor recreation, particularly as the working countryside continues to become more impoverished of beauty and interest. Historic parks, properly restored and managed, could be oases of peace and beauty, and in many areas provide the best opportunity for people to commune with nature.

The task of restoration is complex and difficult. Not only is there a long backlog of maintenance to be tackled, but provision has to be made for future management. There are, though, the stirrings of encouraging signs. Nationally, a number of gardens threatened by neglect or change have been restored, often against all the odds. Painshill in Surrey, Painswick in Gloucestershire, and the National Trust restoration of the Victorian masterpiece, Biddulph Grange, are notable examples. These have all received widespread support from the public, from grant-giving bodies, from charitable trusts, and from the private sector. They have also attracted the attention of the media, which has in turn raised public awareness of our garden heritage.

Popular interest has been reawakened, for example, in walled gardens, 'redundant' features all too often converted into car parks or swimming pools, or filled with housing or office buildings. The recent television series and its best-selling book on the Victorian kitchen garden, introduced by Peter Thoday of Bath University, have been immensely influential. Thoday is currently involved in the restoration of the walled gardens, complete with pineapple pits and gardener's bothy, at Heligan in Cornwall; these, too, have captured the public's imagination. Perhaps the demand for organic food and old flavoursome varieties of fruit and vegetables will help revive a role for these old gardens. The Freeways Trust grows and sells a range of produce in the huge kitchen garden at Leigh Court, for the benefit of its residents.

New hope for old gardens

The movement for the conservation of historic parks and gardens began in earnest with the founding of the Garden History Society in 1965, at a time when general interest was at an all-time low. Begun by garden enthusiasts as a learned society for the research and study of historic gardens, the Garden History Society, with a membership of more than 1,500, is now the country's leading independent campaigner for their protection. This is achieved by involvement in the planning system, presentation of seminars and workshops on a broad range of subjects relating to historic parks and gardens, publications of reports, and a journal of recent research.

In 1978 the National Council for the Conservation of Plants and Gardens (NCCPG) was founded as a charitable trust to conserve ornamental plant cultivars. Not only are old cultivars of value in recreating or restoring period gardens but they are an important genetic resource for plant-breeding programmes, and natural sources of medicinal chemicals. Part of the work of the NCCPG is to establish and maintain national collections of species, hybrids and cultivars within a particular genus. In 1992 Avon held six of these national collections: *Caryopteris* and *Actinidia* at Bristol Zoo; asters at Quarry Farm, Wraxall; *Dodecatheon* at The Manor House, Walton-in-Gordano; *Passiflora* at Greenholm Nurseries, Congresbury; and *Taxus* at Bath University.

One of the greatest difficulties in the conservation of historic parks and gardens was to get them recognised as designed landscapes, as works of art, rather than as natural landscapes – merely a pleasing and fortuitous combination of grass, trees and water. It is a testimony to the eighteenth-century landscapers' art that even owners were often unaware of the efforts that had gone into producing and perfecting a 'natural' Arcadian scene.

The Garden History Society was one of the key lobbyists in promoting public interest in historic parks and gardens, as embodied in the National Heritage Act of 1983. This led to the establishment of a national Register of Parks and Gardens of Special Historic Interest, compiled by English Heritage, which is treated as a 'material consideration' in planning decisions. This means that the historic landscape interest can be weighed against other interests – nature conservation or golf course development, for example – when planners make decisions.

The Register for Avon contained twenty entries when published in 1985; since then a further ten sites have been added as a result of lobbying by the Avon Gardens Trust. However, the Register only records the finest parks and gardens – amounting to about 1,500 nationally. With historic parks and gardens now finally on the conservation agenda, Avon County Council took advantage of Manpower Services Commission funding to launch the Historic Garden Survey through the Avon County Community Environment Scheme (ACCES). Between 1984 and 1988 the survey teams visited more than five hundred sites in the county, and recorded two hundred and eighty as being of historic interest – almost ten times the number in the Register.

The work of the ACCES teams became the foundation of the Avon Gardens Trust, an educational charity set up in 1987 with two objectives: to promote the education of the public about valuable historic parks and gardens, and to promote the preservation, enhancement and re-creation of these parks and gardens. The Trust has now published two editions of the *Avon Gazetteer of Historic Parks and Gardens*, which lists all the recorded sites in the county, with their principal features and conservation designations. It was designed for planners as much as for enthusiasts, and has been incorporated into planning policies in local plans by Bristol City Council, Northavon and Woodspring District Councils, and is used by the other local authorities to guide decision-making.

Increasingly, the Avon Gardens Trust works with other counties in the Association of Gardens Trusts to organise national lobbying on legislation for the protection of historic parks and gardens, and on funding for their restoration.

Protection – and the planning system
In the absence of specific planning controls, historic parks and gardens and their constituent features can be protected through the planning system by a hotch-potch of statutory measures.

Garden buildings and ornaments, for example, may be designated as listed buildings by English Heritage, and will therefore require planning consent for any alterations, development or demolition. However, the greatest enemy of garden buildings is neglect, and planning authorities and English Heritage have unfortunately been reluctant to implement the powers they have available to force owners to repair – even when it involves listed garden buildings in conservation areas.

Gardens may also be scheduled as ancient monuments, but usually only when they contain important and extensive buried features, or earthworks from an early period, such as the sixteenth-century garden at Acton Court in Iron Acton.

About half of the registered sites in Avon are included, either in part or in whole, in conservation areas. In theory these gardens should, like the buildings, be eligible for grants from English Heritage, but in practice the money is not available. Tree preservation orders (TPOs) can be useful for protecting individual trees, clumps, avenues, hedges and belts. In conservation areas, owners are required to obtain consent to fell a tree – as they are to demolish even an unlisted building.

Legislation is, of course, only part of the answer to the conservation of such fragile and dynamic structures as gardens. Raising public awareness of their heritage and amenity value is vital if these unique works of art are to be maintained for the enjoyment of future generations. Only when the value of a garden or park is recognised by the owners or by those who enjoy it, can it be saved. The nature of the value placed on each site will vary: it may be seen as a part of history, local or national; as a work of art; as a place or learning; as a recreational area; or simply as a piece of paradise. By articulating these values as a groundswell of public opinion and concern, the necessary support may be found for both legislation and funding for the conservation of our garden heritage.

An Ill Wind

The great storms which struck the West Country in January and February 1990 were particularly devastating to historic parks and gardens (Plate 35). Historic sites had the greatest proportion of giant and geriatric trees, and the wind was ruthless in their destruction. The government made resources available for storm damage repair, much of it to be targetted at historic parks and gardens on the Register. The work of administering grant-aid was shared between English Heritage, who dealt with the 'outstanding' sites, and the Countryside Commission, which set up a special unit, Task Force Trees, for the purpose.

In the course of clearing up the damage, it became clear that the storms were just the latest event in the decline of designed parks, and that much more than one-for-one replacement of trees was required. The two agencies agreed that initial grants would be made available for urgent clearance work, but further aid would only be given if a detailed restoration plan based on thorough research were produced. Generous grants of 75% of the cost were made available to encourage owners to undertake this full assessment of the sites.

In Avon, the importance of these grants cannot be over-emphasised; they provided the opportunity to move from the defensive protection of parks and gardens into the more positive arena of restoration. Task Force Trees entered into an agency arrangement with Avon County Council and the Avon Gardens Trust to promote the scheme, with the result that far more registered parks and gardens in Avon now have restoration plans than in any other county in England. The production of the plans has been a worthwhile academic exercise in its own right, because the archival, cartographical, pictorial and field surveys undertaken by expert consultants as the basis for restoration plans has been, in many instances, the first thorough research conducted into the landscape history of the sites.

Once the plans have been approved by Task Force Trees and English Heritage, implementation generally follows a similar course of clearance, tree surgery and replanting. One of the principal findings of the restoration plans is the overwhelming need to clear away not just storm damage but self-sown trees and scrub in neglected areas, in order to uncover the historic design and to reopen view corridors and viewpoints. Often the very clear distinction between grass and woods, so characteristic of parks, has become blurred. Clearing back to the fence line can have an instant and astonishing impact in dramatising the landscape design.

The research findings have yet to be systematically analysed, but some points of great interest have already emerged. For example, the work of Humphry Repton at Blaise Castle, Leigh Court, Ashton Court and Oldbury Court has been documented for the first time. At Ashton Court a pencil sketch by Repton was discovered, showing his proposal for a lake south of the mansion. This was never implemented but the research did show that the park's present configuration of grass and trees was Repton's. His design brilliantly connected the various landscape 'cells' of a vast park, by grassy slopes and rides which sweep between the plantations. The area known as the grass-ski slope turns out to be the remains of an elaborate seventeenth-century formal garden, with wide terraces stepping down the hill to a bowling green in front of the mansion.

Blaise is acknowledged as one of Repton's finest and most complete works. His drive from the castellated lodge on Henbury Hill, zigzagging down the valley between hanging woods, is a *tour de force*, making the most of the varied landscape. Apart from being in urgent need of more intensive management, Blaise Castle park is pretty much as Repton left it. Oldbury Court, on the other hand, has fared less well. The involvement of Humphry Repton in the layout of its woods and walks was discovered only recently, and the hanging woods, full of trees dating from his time, are now in urgent need of maintenance and sympathetic replanting. The City Council's restoration plan shows what a dramatic site it once was, making full use of the glen of the River Frome with its picturesque mills and quarries.

The plan for Stoke Park revealed it as a complete and comprehensive layout by Thomas Wright, who designed not only the park and garden buildings but also the 'Jacobean' revival castle. More of a surprise is his probable involvement in the mid eighteenth-century landscaping at Kingsweston, traditionally associated with Capability Brown. The two landscapes Brown designed near Bath, Newton Park and Kelston, were both on older sites. What has emerged here is that Brown did not sweep away all traces of 'cold formality', but preserved the existing avenues and view lines while reworking the areas closest to the house in informal style. Brown was also involved with modifying the landscape at Prior Park, recently taken over by the National Trust. English Heritage has grant-aided the Trust to commission landscape consultants to undertake intensive research into the site's evolution. The findings will guide the Trust's restoration strategy.

Restoration and Reconstruction

Claverton Manor

A replica of George Washington's garden at Mount Vernon in Virginia was constructed in the eighteenth-century park of Claverton Manor by the American Museum in 1961. There is also a colonial herb garden, a fernery, and an arboretum of North American trees planted in the 1960s. An apple arch uses only American varieties and stocks. There are also new borders by Lanning Roper. The site, near Bath, is appropriate, as the original Mount Vernon was embellished with seeds and plants from the area, a local farmer being sent over to help with the planting.

Interestingly, the famous reconstruction of the Governor's Palace and garden in Colonial Williamsburg, also in Virginia, was made possible by the inventories of Norborne Berkeley of Stoke Park, later Lord Botetourt, Governor of Virginia from 1765 to 1768.

The National Trust

The National Trust has been a pioneer in garden restoration. Westbury Court in Gloucestershire was one of their earliest projects. Here, the seventeenth-century formal gardens have been restored, and part of the garden reserved exclusively for plants cultivated in that century. The realisation that historic parks and gardens could attract visitors (and income) in their own right, rather than merely as the setting to a grand house, has improved the quality of grounds maintenance.

The National Trust benefits from a percentage of the funds raised by the National Gardens Scheme, which was started in 1927 to support the Queen's Nursing Institute for district nurses. Through garden open days, organised by owners and volunteers, the Scheme has raised millions of pounds for the Trust and for nursing charities, and has also given millions of visitors the opportunity to admire and learn from gardens of all types. Every year, in March, 'The Yellow Book' is published, listing the gardens that are open to the public. Avon is well represented, with over fifty gardens open on certain days from April to September.

Restoration Projects – trusts, groups, and educational aims
One of the most encouraging aspects of the recent trend towards better care for historic parks and gardens is the increasing involvement of voluntary and community groups. The Stoke Park Restoration Trust was founded in 1989 to act as an umbrella organisation for representatives of the many amenity groups which had expressed concern over the future of Bristol's 'green gateway'. Following the Avon Gardens Trust's restoration of Thomas Wright's Beaufort Memorial (1756) at Stoke Park, the Stoke Park Restoration Trust has restored, in partnership with Stapleton Conservation Society, the walls, piers and pillars of Duchess Gate (1762). Also at Stoke Park (Plate 39), Avon County Council, using the restoration plan produced with grant-aid from Task Force Trees, has restored the wide grass viewing terrace overlooking the park at Sims Hill. It is hoped that this will form part of the footpath network linking Bristol's urban area with the countryside and community forest to the north. The most ambitious restoration project currently underway is the recreation of the 2 1/4-acre/0.9-hectare Duchess Pond to replace the 1768 original which was filled in for the construction of the M32.

Because of the long lead time required for the preparation of restoration plans, work on the ground under the grant schemes in Avon is just beginning to gather momentum. The Freeways Trust has finished clearing the self-sown sycamore, ash, rhododendron and laurel from Repton's pleasure grounds at Leigh Court, and has carved out the walks to their historic design, in preparation for replanting. Kingswood School and Beckford's Tower Trust, in partnership with the Bath Preservation Trust, are working on different parts of Beckford's Ride, where the long-term aim is to secure again a picturesque walk from Lansdown Crescent to Beckford's Tower at the top of the ridge.

At Clevedon Court the Wildlife Trust, again with help from Task Force Trees, has repaired the three ornamental stone bridges which were essential to the mid nineteenth-century wood walks laid out by Lady Elton. The paths are also being restored by the Trust to provide high quality public access to what has become a nature reserve. Here, the ornamental character and purpose of the woods has been recognised, and the Wildlife Trust is safeguarding that aspect in its wildlife management of the site.

The Friends of Blaise have been resolute in their lobbying for the proper detailed care that the landscape at Blaise Castle warrants. The City's financial problems have seriously affected maintenance, not only of the buildings, such as Nash's exquisite orangery, but also of the woodlands themselves. The Friends have also raised thousands of pounds towards the repair of paths and the orangery, and have been enthusiastic consultees in the preparation of the City Council's restoration plan for the site.

At Thornbury Castle, now a hotel, the current owner, Baron Porthleven, recently commissioned a historic survey and restoration plan. The survey unearthed (literally) evidence for the Tudor arrangement of walks and flower beds, and it is hoped that these may be recreated for the benefit of guests.

Voluntary groups have played an important part in campaigns to improve town gardens. The Clifton and Hotwells Improvement Society has restored the walls around the Mall Gardens and is set to improve the Lookout, a public area for viewing Clifton Suspension Bridge. The local community has been involved in the planning and construction of Eastville Park Community Garden inside the walls of a disused open-air swimming bath. The Bristol 'Improve Our Parks' campaign has lobbied successfully for decent children's playgrounds, securing improvements to the parks at Arno's Court, Charles Place in Hotwells, Felix Road in Easton, and Windmill Hill City Farm. The campaign estimates that a total of £4 million is needed to bring the city's playgrounds up to standard. Local campaigns have also centred round the need for improvements to Canford Park at Westbury-on-Trym, and the unusable play area under the Cumberland Basin flyover. In Weston-super-Mare the Seroptomists, a business club for women, intends to restore the Garden of Fragrance in Grove Park, which was laid out in 1958 for the blind.

While fresh air and exercise have long been considered important, the value of rich and diverse designed landscapes to the education of children has only recently come onto the agenda. The gang mowers so beloved of local education authorities, and the lack of funds for trained gardeners, have led to school grounds being among the most barren of green deserts. Recognising the poverty and depressing nature of these surroundings, the Learning through Landscapes Trust aims to enrich and diversify school grounds as rewarding playgrounds to which children can relate positively. It promotes their use at the same time as outdoor classrooms, providing an exciting resource for a range of subjects from art to zoology. The Wildlife Trust and parents' associations have carried out projects in school gardens; and the Avon Gardens Trust has planted trees and a shrub border with bulbs at Dr Bells School in Fishponds, as well as preparing a planting scheme for 2,000 trees at Whitefield School, where the first trees were planted by the school in 1992.

Local authorities

In 1984 the growth of interest in the archaeology and reconstruction of early gardens prompted Bristol City Council to lay out the Tudor 'privy' garden at the sixteenth-century Red Lodge, one of the city's museums; and at 4 The Circus in Bath, the Council sponsored the project to construct a period garden for the 1758 house.

No documentary evidence existed for the original garden in the Circus, and the Bath Archaeological Society undertook an excavation of the site to see what it might reveal. The result has been a landmark in garden history. The house had been altered, and the garden redesigned, in the nineteenth century, but underneath about 12 inches/30 centimetres of clay and topsoil the original garden was found to have survived almost intact. It has been restored, using a planting scheme drawn up by John Harvey of the Garden History Society, and with the help of Lorna McRobie and Stan Hitt.

More recently, public spending limits have severely affected local councils, and in particular their ability to manage and maintain parks. Because open spaces are not a statutory provision, they inevitably absorb a disproportionate share of cuts. However, the demand from the public for good quality parks and gardens, the availability of grants for registered sites, and the upsurge in academic interest are bringing about a reappraisal of priorities.

Bath City Council took advantage of grants from Task Force Trees to have restoration plans drawn up by John Phibbs for its two registered public parks, Royal Victoria Park and Sydney Gardens. All the trees in Royal Victoria Park have been identified and surveyed for health, and a lengthy programme of felling and tree surgery has been completed in preparation for replanting to the nineteenth-century design. At Sydney Gardens some clearance work has been undertaken, but it is hoped that the money can be found for a complete restoration in time for the bicentenary of the garden's opening in 1995.

Bristol City Council has recently completed a restructuring of the way it manages its parks and open spaces. The historic parks at Ashton Court, Blaise Castle, Oldbury Court and Castle Park (although, inexplicably, not Kingsweston) have been put, with the museums and art gallery, under the Heritage Directorate. It is hoped that this will ensure that the interests of the historic landscape designs will be given priority over other demands – though not to their exclusion.

Some good work has already been done by the Council at Ashton Court in removing scrubby areas from the wood margins and replanting some of the oaks that have been lost over the years. One of the urgent jobs identified in the restoration plan, and recently completed, was to remove self-sown sycamore and ash from Clerkencombe Wood, where they were overshadowing ancient oak pollards. Unfortunately, many have already died, but the two hundred and eighty survivors are a unique collection in Avon of rare old trees, and a major wildlife resource (Fig. 4). It is hoped to bring this area back into the deer park and re-establish it as wood pasture, with new oaks pollarded at the appropriate stage. Further clearance of view corridors should put back the flow of grassland from one part of the landscape to another, reversing the trend of woodland creeping out from the margins and coalescing, which threatens to break the park up visually into disconnected fragments. Renovation of the historic design here, as elsewhere, is important not as a narrow academic exercise but in order to maintain the beauty of the landscape for all. Left to nature, it would lose the quality for which it is so prized.

The restoration plan also drew attention to Sir Greville Smyth's sequoias. Those nearest the mansion are now overwhelming and belittling the grandeur of the architecture, as well as threatening the structural stability of the ha-ha. The problem of these magnificent but badly sited trees needs to be addressed before long.

As Repton found when he laid out Blaise Castle park, clearance was the urgent task before planting could begin, and the experience of producing restoration plans has confirmed his remarks on the importance of the 'judicious use of the axe' to reveal the 'Genius of the place'. English Heritage has earmarked funds for a Bristol City Council implementation of the restoration plan that will let the air back into the woods, rides and walks, drying them out and making for a more pleasant experience. Some of the problems here of scrub on the steep slopes are the same as at Stoke Park, where the effect is to weaken the landscape design by obscuring the drama of the topography. The art of planting trees on hill-tops and in the valleys, with grass on the slopes between to exaggerate the changes of level, was perfected in the eighteenth century, and can be seen in contemporary illustrations.

Oldbury Court needs the same sort of attention. The woodland walks in the Frome Valley are littered with, and in places blocked by, fallen trees. All the big trees, mostly beech and oak, are of the same age, dating back to Repton's visit in 1800. The beech require a programme of phased renewal, while large areas by the riverside, and blocked views from the paths, need to be cleared. The haphazard planting of anything and everything in the parkland next to the drive needs to be carefully sorted out, and there should be a programme of planting parkland trees and perimeter belts. There is hope that its historic character could be reclaimed.

Conclusion

This book has demonstrated the richness of the garden heritage in the county of Avon. We are fortunate that it has been so well documented and that so many individuals and organisations are prepared to work towards its preservation and restoration. The conservation of historic parks and gardens is not just an exercise in nostalgia. It must be remembered that for two hundred years the English were absolutely obsessed by landscape gardening. Repton, at the height of his powers, declared: 'All England shall be a garden'. That is a vision that was forgotten in the post-war enthusiasm for all things modern. We have had a chance to ponder on what was lost during that period, and the poverty of its legacy. Towns and cities have become dominated by office blocks and motor cars. Town centres die when the shops shut. Decaying parks are shunned by all except those with nothing better to do. The regeneration of parks and gardens could be a powerful symbol of civic pride restored. Our parks and gardens were built for pleasure; they need our attention in order that they may give pleasure once again.

Bibliography

Robert Atkyns, *The Ancient and Present State of Glostershire* (London, 1712)

Mavis Batey and David Lambert, *The English Garden Tour* (London, 1990)

Bath City Council, *Bath Landscape Strategy* (Bath, 1988)

Reginald Blomfield, *The Formal Garden in England* (London, 1912)

P. Bright, *Dr Richard Bright* (Bristol, 1983)

Bristol City Council, *Open Space in Bristol* (Bristol, 1984)

> *Draft Policy for the Preservation and Enhancement of Stoke Park/Purdown* (Bristol, 1986)
>
> *Brentry Conservation Area Draft Proposals* (Bristol, 1988)
>
> *Policy of the Preservation and Enhancement of Stoke Park/Purdown* (Bristol, 1990)

George Carter, Patrick Goode, Kedrun Laurie, *Humphry Repton: Landscape Gardener 1752-1818* (Norwich, 1982)

John Chilcott, *Descriptive History of Bristol* (Bristol, 1844)

John Collinson, *History and Antiquities of Somersetshire*, 3 vols (Bath, 1791)

R. Cooke, *West Country Houses* (Bristol, 1952)

H. Conway, *People's Parks* (Cambridge, 1991)

R. Desmond, *Bibliography of British Gardens* (Winchester, 1984)

Celia Fiennes, *The Journeys of Celia Fiennes*, ed. Christopher Morris (London, 1947)

L. Fleming and A. Gore, *The English Garden* (London, 1988)

Stewart Harding, *Repton in Avon* (Avon Gardens Trust, 1989)

> 'The Wizard's Lodge Rediscovered', *Avon Gardens Trust Newsletter*, Summer (Bristol, 1989)
>
> 'The Great Hospital Bazaar', *The Planner*, Vol 75, No 33 (London, 1989)
>
> *Proposals for the Restoration of Stoke Park* (Bristol, 1990)
>
> 'Parks and Gardens of the Frome Valley', *Avon Gardens Trust Newsletter*, Spring (Bristol, 1992)
>
> 'Stoke Park', *Old House Gardens*, March (London, 1992)
>
> 'Task Force Trees in the South-west', *The Garden History Society Newsletter*, No 38, Summer (Old Woodstock, 1993)

Stewart Harding and David Lambert, 'The Genius of Thomas Wright', *Bristol Illustrated*, October (Bristol, 1987)

> 'Saving the Wizard's Landscape', *Country Life*, April 14 (London, 1988)
>
> 'Lodge by Thomas Wright?', *Country Life*, March 2 (London, 1989)
>
> *Gazetteer of Historic Parks and Gardens in Avon*, 2nd Edition (Bristol, 1991)

E. Harris, *Thomas Wright: Arbours and Grottoes* (London 1979)

G.S. Hart, *Ham Green* (Pill, 1990)

John Harvey, *Mediaeval Gardens* (London, 1990)

Bibliography

Historic Buildings and Monuments Commission for England, *Register of Parks and Gardens of Special Historic Interest* (London, 1984–7)

John Dixon Hunt and Peter Willis ed., *The Genius of the Place* (London, 1975)

E. Hyams, *The English Garden* (London, 1964)

D. Jacques, *Georgian Gardens: the Reign of Nature* (London, 1983)

G. Jekyll, *Wall and Water Gardens* (London, 1901)

'Changes of Fashion', *Nineteenth Century*, August (London, 1928)

Geoffrey Jellicoe et al, *Oxford Companion to Gardens* (Oxford, 1986)

H. Johnson, *The Principles of Gardening* (London, 1980)

Nicholas Kingsley, *The Country Houses of Gloucestershire*, vols 1 and 2 (Cheltenham and Chichester, 1989-92)

David Lambert and Stewart Harding, 'The Thomas Wright Landscape at Stoke Park', *Georgian Group Newsletter*, No 6, Spring (London, 1988)

'Stoke Park and the Wizard of Durham', *Bath Preservation Trust Newsletter*, May (Bath, 1988)

K. Laurie, 'Interview with Her Grace The Duchess of Beaufort', *Avon Gardens Trust Newsletter*, No 3, Summer (Bristol, 1988)

Anthony Mitchell, *The Park and Garden at Dyrham* (London, 1977)

L. McRobie and S. Harding, *Historic Parks and Gardens in the County of Avon* (Bristol, 1988)

Tim Mowl, *To Build the Second City* (Bristol, 1991)

Bristol: Last Age of the Merchant Princes (Bristol, 1991)

Elizabethan and Jacobean Style (London, 1993)

'Henry Edmund Goodridge and a new Florence in the West', *Georgian Group in the West Newsletter*

Palladian Bridges (Bath, 1993)

Tim Mowl and Brian Earnshaw, *Trumpet at a Distant Gate* (London, 1985)

J. Nelson, *A History of Manor Park Hospital* (Bristol, 1982)

J. Nolen, *The Art of Landscape Gardening by Humphry Repton Esq* (Boston & New York, 1907)

Nikolaus Pevsner, *North Somerset and Bristol* (Harmondsworth, 1973)

D. Pilcher, *The Regency Style* (London, 1947)

K. Powell and M. Watson-Smith, *Hospitals: a Suitable Case for Treatment* (London, 1987)

Historic Hospitals at Risk (London, 1990)

G. Priest and P. Cobb, *The Battle for Bristol* (Bristol, 1980)

J.V. Punter, *Design Control in Bristol 1940-1990* (Bristol, 1990)

Oliver Rackham, *The History of the Countryside* (London, 1986)

Trees and Woodland in the British Landscape (London, 1990)

Samuel Rudder, *A New History of Gloucestershire* (Cirencester, 1779)

James Russell, 'The Hanging Gardens of Crew's Hole', *Avon Gardens Trust Newsletter*, No 9, Autumn (Bristol, 1991)

John Sales, *West Country Gardens* (Gloucester, 1981)

J.A. Smith, *Pavilions in Peril* (London, 1986)

Mary Stacey, *The Protection of Historic Parks and Gardens in the Planning System*, Bristol Polytechnic Department of Town and Country Planning Working Paper WP29 (Bristol, 1992)

Mary Stacey and Stewart Harding, 'Following the Garden Path', *Planning* No 944, Nov 15 (Gloucester, 1991)

Roy Strong, *The Renaissance Garden in England* (London, 1979)

Dorothy Stroud, *Humphry Repton* (London, 1962)

    Capability Brown (London, 1975)

M. Symes, *The English Rococo Garden* (Princes Risborough, 1991)

Anthea Taigel and Tom Williamson, *Parks and Gardens* (London, 1993)

David Verey, *Gloucestershire*, 2 vols. (Harmondsworth, 1979-80)

E. Wilson and S. Harding, 'Batheaston Project', *Avon Conservation News*, No 27, March (Bristol, 1988)

Index